Why Taiwan Matters

Why Taiwan Matters

A Short History of a Small Island That Will Dictate Our Future

KERRY BROWN

ST. MARTIN'S PRESS
NEW YORK

First published in the United States by St. Martin's Press, an imprint of
St. Martin's Publishing Group

www.stmartins.com

The Library of Congress Cataloging-in-Publication Data is available upon request.

ISBN 978-1-250-36209-4 (hardcover)
ISBN 978-1-250-36210-0 (ebook)

Our books may be purchased in bulk for promotional, educational, or
business use. Please contact your local bookseller or the Macmillan Corporate
and Premium Sales Department at 1-800-221-7945, extension 5442, or by
email at MacmillanSpecialMarkets@macmillan.com.

First U.S. Edition: 2025

10 9 8 7 6 5 4 3 2 1

Dedicated to the memory of Frank Charles Clark
1936–1993

Contents

Timeline

230 CE   One of the earliest mentions of Taiwan island in Chinese-language sources.

1349   First account of Taiwan by a Chinese visitor, Wang Dayuan. From this period, settlers from the mainland arrive to live on the island.

1620s   Settlement of Taiwan by Dutch and Spanish. The Dutch start to construct Fort Zeelandia in 1625.

1642   Control of Taiwan by the Dutch, after forcing the total withdrawal of the Spanish.

1644   Collapse of the Ming Dynasty and establishment of the Qing Dynasty. Rebel forces under Zheng Chenggong make Taiwan a stronghold.

1661   The Kangxi emperor comes to the throne at the age of six. In the following sixty years of his reign, there is a major expansion of Qing-controlled territory.

1662   Zheng's forces defeat the Dutch and expel them from Taiwan. The anti-Qing Tungning Dynasty is established under Zheng, who dies shortly afterwards and is succeeded by his son, Zheng Jing.

1683   Qing conquest of Taiwan and end of the Tungning Dynasty. It is made a prefecture of Fujian province for the next 205 years.

1721   Start of a series of rebellions, first by Chinese settlers and then by Taiwanese indigenous peoples; parts of Taiwan island are marked off as beyond Chinese control. The rebellions continue throughout the eighteenth and early nineteenth centuries.

1860   Convention of Beijing after the Second Anglo-Chinese War opens up parts of Taiwan to foreign trade.

1884–5   French attempts to annex Taiwan by force are repelled by the Qing army.

1887   Taiwan upgraded from a prefecture to a separate province with its own governor and some autonomy from China.

1895   Chinese forces beaten in the Sino-Japanese War. Treaty of Shimonoseki cedes Taiwan to Japanese colonial rule until 1945.

1911–12 Collapse of the Qing Dynasty and establishment of the Republic of China.

1930   Uprising against the Japanese by indigenous Atayal Taiwanese met with violent reprisals.

1943   Cairo Declaration agrees that, in the event of Allied victory in the Second World War, all Chinese territories seized by Japan will be returned to the Chinese government, including Taiwan.

1945   Defeat of the Japanese, and retrocession of Taiwan to the Republic of China. It becomes a province with its own governor.

1946–9   Chinese Civil War between the Nationalists under Chiang Kai-shek and the Communists under Mao Zedong, during which 2 million people flee the mainland for Taiwan.

1947   28 February Incident: Chinese governor Chen Yi violently represses a local protest. Forces arrive from the mainland and instigate a reign of terror.

1949   Defeat of the Nationalists in China and relocation of the Republic of China's government under Chiang Kai-shek to

Taiwan. Martial law is declared, lasting until 1987. Foundation of the People's Republic of China in Beijing.

1950   Attempts by the Communists to launch an invasion of Taiwan are permanently postponed after the North Koreans invade South Korea, starting the Korean War. United Nations forces wage war against the North Koreans, who are massively supported by the Chinese. As a result of the war, the US commits to Taiwan's defence.

1955   Clashes between Chinese and Taiwanese forces (known as the First Strait Crisis). US–Taiwan mutual defence treaty, signed in Taipei at the end of 1954, is implemented.

1958   Second Strait Crisis: People's Republic forces trying to take Kinmen (sometimes called Jinmin or Quemoy) and Matsu islands are repulsed.

1971   Taiwan loses its seat at the United Nations after a majority of countries vote for the People's Republic to replace it representing China.

1972   Visit by US President Richard Nixon to Beijing, and signing of the Shanghai Communiqué which 'acknowledges' that there is only one China, and that Taiwan is part of China.

1975   Death of Chiang Kai-shek. Succeeded as president of Taiwan by his son, Chiang Ching-kuo, in 1978.

1979   US shifts formal diplomatic recognition from Taiwan to the People's Republic of China. US Congress passes the Taiwan Relations Act, stipulating that it must be consulted over Taiwan's security.

1980   Aftermath of the Kaohsiung Incident in southern Taiwan: heavy prison sentences are handed out to the leaders of the pro-democracy protests.

1987   Martial law lifted, after thirty-eight years. Democratic Progressive Party legalized and starts contesting elections.

1988   Death of Chiang Ching-kuo. Succeeded as leader of the Nationalist Party by Lee Teng-hui.

1991   First fully democratic elections for the Legislative Assembly. The presidency remains appointed rather than directly elected.

1995   Visit of President Lee Teng-hui to the US to give a speech results in Chinese military exercises in the strait, and the US deploying two aircraft carriers to the region.

1996   First presidential election on the principle of universal franchise for all Taiwanese adults over twenty-one. Lee Teng-hui wins an overwhelming majority.

2000   First election of a Democratic Progressive Party candidate, Chen Shui-bian, as president.

2008   Nationalist Party returns to power under President Ma Ying-jeou.

2010   Economic Cooperation Framework Agreement between Taiwan and China, resulting in direct air, postal and tourist links, and free trade of some goods.

2012   Ma Ying-jeou re-elected as president. Xi Jinping comes to power as leader of the Communist Party in China.

2014   Sunflower Protests force the Ma administration to abandon plans for a common investment agreement with China.

2015   Ma Ying-jeou and Xi Jinping are the first leaders of the Republic of China and the People's Republic of China to meet in person (in Singapore).

2016   Tsai Ing-wen, the Democratic Progressive Party candidate, is elected president.

2019   Protests in Hong Kong over a new national security law and proposals for extradition legislation subjecting Hong Kong and Taiwan nationals to the Chinese justice system – seen in Taiwan as the end of any possibility of using the 'One Country, Two Systems' rubric to manage Taiwan's status.

2020   Tsai Ing-wen re-elected as president. The 'Safeguarding National Security in the Hong Kong Special Administrative Region' law is passed by Beijing.

2020–23   COVID-19 pandemic: Taiwan experiences one of the lowest mortality rates in the world, despite never imposing a national lockdown.

2022   Nancy Pelosi, Speaker of the US House of Representatives, becomes the highest-ranked American official to visit Taiwan since 1996.

2024   William Lai Ching-te, the Democratic Progressive Party candidate, is elected president.

Taiwan and the Taiwan Strait

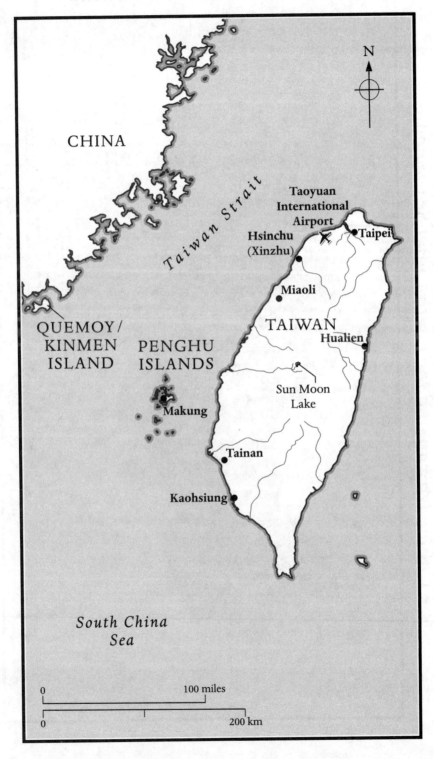

China, Taiwan and the South China Sea region

First island chain

0   1,000 miles

0   2,000 km

Pacific Ocean

PHILIPPINES

TAIWAN

Shanghai

Beijing

CHINA

Xiamen

HONG KONG

A Note on Terms

Discussion of Taiwan is beset by the problem of how to refer to the key players. 'Taiwan' was originally the name of the main island (one of more than 160) that today constitutes the 'Republic of China' (ROC). The Republic of China has been in existence since 1911–12 when the Chinese Qing Dynasty collapsed. After the Civil War in China between 1946 and 1949, the Republic's government moved to Taiwan island, and from that point was largely known as the 'Republic of China on Taiwan'. While this is its official name, the shorter 'Taiwan', or 'the island', are used in this book for ease and clarity.

Before the Civil War, the Republic of China was governed by the Nationalist Party. It is often referred to by its Chinese name: the 'Guomindang' (GMD), in the modern transliteration system from Chinese to English (called Pinyin); or the 'Kuomintang' (KMT), according to an older transcription method. In this book, 'Nationalist Party' is the sole term used. The victor in the Civil War was the Communist Party of China (CPC), which created the 'People's Republic of China' (PRC) in 1949. It continues to rule the mainland today. In this book, any of 'People's Republic of China', 'PRC', 'China' or 'the mainland' are the terms used.

There is a rich and complex history of other terms used to refer to Taiwan in English-language material. 'Formosa' is the term used in some of the earliest literature. 'Free China' was one expression deployed in the past, presumably to distinguish Taiwan from the 'unfree China' – as people saw it – that existed on the other side of the 130 kilometre stretch of water called 'the strait'. For the Olympic Games, Taiwanese athletes march under the curious title of 'Chinese Taipei', something enforced by mainland imperatives so as not to confer any hint of recognized sovereignty. In the case of the World Trade Organization, Taiwan was able to join it in 2001, only a few minutes after the People's Republic (despite technically qualifying some years earlier), but as a 'customs territory'. The British Broadcasting Corporation (BBC) and other media outlets call Taiwan a 'self-governing island'. On some websites, to the irritation of many, Taiwan is downgraded to a 'province'. Others label it a 'de facto independent state'. Taiwanese proudly speak of being inhabitants of a 'jewel island'. The more military-minded of them have called the place 'an unsinkable aircraft carrier', or a 'shrimp caught between two whales'.

In this book, Taiwan is sometimes referred to as a 'country'. I've used this word, not because I assume per se that Taiwan is a country, but out of respect to the many Taiwanese I know who believe the place where they live is a nation, and that it should be accorded that status. I've seen the humiliation and hurt that Taiwanese feel abroad when they encounter people or places that deny the existence of where they come from, despite knowing all too well that it is real, even if that is contested by its neighbour. As will become clear, I am not an activist supporter for Taiwan independence, and my use of 'country' should not be read as such. It is simply a recognition of the term that many of those people at the very heart of this issue use – the Taiwanese themselves.

Introduction

What does it mean to be Taiwanese today? To see the name of the place where you live figure in so many news reports, most of them stating that if there is a Third World War, this is where it will start? To have think tanks, media commentators and politicians speak about you as a 'problem'? To be saluted as one of the world's key economies because your country produces the most advanced semiconductors, which the rest of the planet relies upon? To know that, despite this, 90 per cent of the leaders of those other countries don't actually recognize your home as a country at all? And that, above all, you are seen as sitting – through accident of birth – at the heart of arguably the greatest geopolitical challenge of the twenty-first century?

To be Taiwanese in the twenty-first century means that the outside world sees you as part of a matter that needs to be 'managed', a conundrum to be 'solved', a potential flashpoint that needs to be 'contained'. You are involved in something many people, particularly if they are other governments, try to keep 'ambiguous' in order to preserve the current status quo, because they fear what might happen if anyone dares to question it. To be Taiwanese these days means to have a stronger feeling than most people in the world that your fate is not entirely in your own hands. All it needs is one American president to say they recognize Taiwan as a country, or one Chinese leader to say they want Taiwan to return to their fold immediately, and your life will be turned upside down. Being Taiwanese has many meanings. But one thing that most people who are citizens of this island wish they had more of is normality. For the situation concerning Taiwan and its status is anything but normal.

I am not Taiwanese. But for more than thirty years I have dealt with what is euphemistically called 'the Chinese-speaking World', within which China and Taiwan sit alongside one another. I have ended up with a complex set of experiences and interpretations of what Taiwan means. They arise from my many visits to the island since the turn of the millennium, and from my friendships with people in and from Taiwan. And because most of my professional life has been spent researching and writing about Taiwan's partner in this issue: China.

I often feel as if I have ended up with two distinct brains. One I use when I go to the People's Republic of China (PRC), a country whose 1.4 billion strong population constitutes a fifth of humanity. For decades, I've listened to the opinions, histories, attitudes and ideas about Taiwan expressed by Chinese officials, friends and colleagues. Often these occur at interminable public occasions, such as formal banquets with those that work in the administration, or government-supported conferences and seminars. Sometimes they crop up in the middle of totally unrelated informal conversations. I'm told that Taiwan *is* China, that it has always been part of China. With a stern, admonishing look, people tell me that it needs to come back to China, and that outsiders had better keep out of the matter. At the beginning of my career, before I knew much of the history of why these two places today have the relationship they do, I could tell that this was something that people in China felt extremely strongly about. They had a limited appetite for hearing the opinions about this issue of any outsider like me, especially when they ran contrary to what they themselves believed.

But I had the reverse experience in Taiwan. It was like stepping across some magical threshold from one order of reality into another, where everything was instantaneously turned upside down. Those opinions and ideas about the island that were made across the waters were spurious, people told me. But, they quickly added, they were claims made by a bully. They would go on to argue that China was a place that Taiwan had never really belonged to, but with which it had had merely a loose, sporadic association in the past.

As I have travelled back and between these two environments over the years, I have had to acknowledge more and more that Taiwan is indeed different – though the crucial issue is to what extent. Sometimes I feel like I am teetering on the edge of accepting that it is, in fact, a completely separate place. But then the realist in me starts arguing that – for now at least – there is a link with the far larger and more populous country across the strait that can't be ignored, because of the consequences that might follow if it is. Feeling perpetually uncertain, and beset by doubts about the strength of my own position, I imagine I have become a little like the Taiwanese themselves.

I first went to Taiwan in 2000, when I was based in Beijing as a diplomat at the British Embassy. In those days, Taiwan really did feel like the 'renegade' province it was labelled by the People's Republic. There were no direct flights. I had to go via the special territory of Hong Kong (part of China but, as we will see in more detail later, enjoying an unusual status after its return by the British to Chinese rule in 1997), which added hours to the journey. Even on a first visit, Taiwan somehow felt more intimate and easier to relate to than the vastness of the mainland I had come from. The capital, Taipei, had none of the massive, open boulevards of China's centre of government, Beijing. The island was a hard place to classify. The year

I had spent in Japan a decade earlier made me alert to the very distinctive aesthetics of that country: often simple, almost austere and sparse (Zen gardens come to mind, and the pure, clear lines of Japanese architecture). Taiwan carried a hint of this, with its tatami mat floors in older housing, the style of some of its buildings, and its little streams of water flowing beside streets. It had the same profusion of small shops and eateries in tiny alleys that I remembered from Japan, sometimes with sliding doors at the entrance and red paper lanterns hanging from the eaves.

The issue of Taiwan arose from the ruins of the Second World War. What was then a unified Republic of China in effect split in two after the three-year Civil War. The defeated Nationalists, who had ruled the country up to 1949, fled to a part of the territory they had governed since 1945, after taking it back from half a century of Japanese colonial control: Taiwan island. There they continued their regime. The Communist victors on the vast mainland created a new regime, the People's Republic of China. However, both sides claimed that they were the legitimate government of the once-united state, and that the other were usurpers. In the beginning, at least, both vowed to one day achieve reunification.

The conflict that resulted from this split formed one strand of the Cold War through the 1950s and into the 1970s. It pitched an ally of the West against a country run by Communists (even though the Chinese proved highly idiosyncratic Marxists and fell out with their Soviet Union patrons in the late 1950s). Any hopes of an immediate resolution, in which one side prevailed, steadily faded. Over the 1970s, largely led by politicians such as Richard Nixon in Washington and Mao Zedong in Beijing, a framework was painstakingly constructed, which recognized only one China, and fudged the issue of what precisely this meant, in order to manage if not resolve this division while it endured. It meant that everyone could work around the dispute, have relations with either party and not need to decisively choose sides. This was the ultimate diplomatic example of having one's cake and eating it.

Such a situation was deliberately riddled with ambiguity. The simple term 'China', for instance, could either mean 'Republic of China' (Taiwan) or 'People's Republic of China' (the Communist mainland). Games were played with words so that people 'acknowledged' the position of either entity – Taiwan or China – without ever committing themselves to saying if they actually agreed with what was being said. For all the inelegance of this strict focus on semantics, it at least preserved the peace. Unlike many other global conflicts, the dispute between China and Taiwan over the latter's status has not, so far, led to war or outright conflict, testifying to the usefulness of all this playing around with words.

Another reason for the absence of overt conflict is the position of key third parties, of whom the United States is the most important, and the ways they have, up till now, restrained risky attempts at resolution by the two protagonists either side of the strait. Enjoying a trade and political relationship today with both Taiwan and China, the US has achieved this refereeing role by creating a policy of 'strategic ambiguity'. This implies strong interest and commitment by Washington to the security of Taiwan, but no cast-iron promises about what it might do should China ever decide on a full-on assault. The fact that no one knows how America would respond were something drastic to happen has made everyone cautious about trying to force a resolution. It has avoided Washington being manipulated by Taipei and curbed the more impetuous and zealous instincts of others.

For more than four decades, from the 1970s until the early 2020s, this position of ambiguity has preserved at least some boundaries within which Taiwan's status has remained untampered. The island under this protective umbrella has continued to travel along its own distinct path, becoming a democracy and enjoying relative self-determination. But as we look to the future, the Taiwan issue is likely to become increasingly vexed. All the painstaking diplomatic work of the past few decades is under pressure like never before. Key elements of the situation are changing, from the economic and military capacity of China to the rising sense of unique identity within Taiwan itself and the posture of the US. The question of whether the issue of Taiwan will continue to be manageable or will serve as the catalyst for a conflict that could escalate and threaten the rest of the world is becoming more and more urgent. Many worry that the possibility of war is now far likelier than at any time in the last half-century, with Taiwan Foreign Minister Joseph Wu declaring in 2023 that a conflict by 2027 was something 'we need to be serious about'.[1]

One major change prompting these concerns is the way that Chinese power and nationalist ambitions have risen in recent years. Beijing's newly acquired economic capacity is increasingly proving to be a game changer. Up to the 1990s, the People's Republic could express its claims for reunification forcefully but had limited capacity to do anything about them. It had neither the technology nor the military equipment and the financial resources. Today, all that has changed. China is the world's second-largest economy, has the largest navy (in terms of number of vessels, though for the most technologically advanced assets, such as nuclear submarines, the US is still way ahead) and ranks after only the US in terms of military expenditure. It can think about doing things that were never an option in the past. Now, it has the motivation *and* the means. The question for many is no longer whether China can actually do anything, but when it will act.

One result of this change in China's situation is a worrying number of people who believe the West needs to respond by pushing back. This would involve scrapping the ambiguity over Taiwan's status in the face of China's more overtly aggressive and threatening position. In America, in particular, politicians have increasingly moved towards far stronger and clearer expressions of willingness to defend Taiwan. A few have even suggested full recognition of the island's independence. However well intended this demonstration of solidarity is, it risks ramping up the very resolve of the government in Beijing that it is meant to counter. This is because it appears to lead to the one outcome that China has stated categorically it will take any measure to avoid – a separate Taiwan nation. Putting these two standpoints beside each other, it is easy to see how perilously close the world is to outright military escalation.

It may be that our best approach is to admit that we are playing for time. We are all like an audience watching a play where the protagonist looks to be in an impossible trap, waiting for a brilliant twist that delivers them from disaster. Long term, there are hints of developments that might give us hope. Somewhere, somehow, the key factors that dictate the problem and make it so intractable today will change – the priorities of the leaders in China, or the thinking in the rest of the world about big issues like sovereignty and identity. One of the few bright spots in this scenario is the remarkable dynamism of China and Taiwan themselves. Unexpected change should not be dismissed out of hand, because in some spheres (such as the rapid economic growth in both places over the last decades that has had such a material effect on people's lives) it has already happened.

But we have to be absolutely vigilant today. We have to remember that this issue remains volatile, unpredictable and potentially highly destructive. In faded lettering, worn by time, but still stamped across the front of the Taiwan issue is the label 'Highly Dangerous: Handle with Care'. We need to be clear about precisely why the label was put there in the first place, and understand with real clarity what the mismanagement of this issue – by Beijing, Taipei, Washington or anyone else – will mean for the region and for the rest of the world. If this matter gets out of hand, it will have economic, security and diplomatic consequences for everyone. This book will contemplate that scenario and how it might unfold.

A great deal of ink has been spilled over this issue. Taiwan is many things, but underanalysed is not one of them. Despite this, the vast majority of conferences and symposia, and many of the reports on and studies of the island, have taken a wholly external perspective. I have been present at many of these events. They talk of Taiwan's foreign relations, and the responses of key partners like China and the US. But it is as though Taiwan's domestic world does not exist. It is as if someone has described in great detail and with immense care the outside of a box, without thinking to look inside it.

In this short book, I will reverse that approach and plot a kind of journey from the inside out. I will begin by asking who the Taiwanese are, how they live, and how they identify themselves. 'Taiwanese' and 'Chinese' have a close relationship, but it is a layered, complex one, and one that has clearly changed over the past decades. The question today is whether being Taiwanese relates to China in a way that is similar to a resident of New York saying they are a New Yorker and also an American (and therefore a citizen of a larger entity they recognize they belong to and have obligations towards), or more like a

British person saying they are also European (a far looser, more distant relationship).

Crucial to this question of identity is the remarkable history of this island and its 160-plus far smaller satellites. Learning about their past naturally helps us understand how Taiwan has ended up in a situation where there are such fierce arguments and conflicting opinions about how it should define itself. This history sometimes appears to offer the evidence – if cherry-picked – for anyone to prove their point. The Chinese see it as testifying to their unique claims over the place. Many Taiwanese, on the contrary, see it as supporting their view of themselves as autonomous and unique. Plenty of observers might feel that it provides a narrative that is inconclusive and variegated, justifying their own ambiguity on the matter. Either way, an understanding of the past is crucial to appreciating the present predicament Taiwan is in, if only to show how complex that quandary is and how unwise it would be to jump to quick conclusions.

Taiwan is important not just for its past but because of where it sits today, across vast ideological and cultural tectonic fault lines as potentially destructive as the geological ones which produce its all too frequent earthquakes. Taiwan's recent history has followed a path towards democracy and liberalism, unlike that of its Chinese neighbour, still pursuing its authoritarian Communist system. Democratic reform has produced remarkable stories from the Taiwanese people involved, and equally remarkable outcomes for their country, with a journey that has taken them from the Nationalist Party's monopoly on power to the dynamic multiparty system that exists today. The landmark events in achieving this political change in just a few years in the late 1980s and early 1990s are important to bear in mind. But it also needs to be remembered that as much as Taiwan took administrative ideas and models of governance from the outside world, it transformed them into something with values and mindsets that are distinctly local. Today, Taiwan is a place of vibrant hybridity, a place that no more belongs to the West than to China, but needs to be understood on its own terms.

Nor should we neglect the profound wider implications of Taiwan's political journey. Becoming a democracy has not just changed the way that the island is governed, it has also raised the profile and the significance of the argument it has with the mainland. Were Taiwan still to have the same one-party system that governed it from the 1940s to the 1980s, its current predicament would not attract anything like the sympathy and support it does from the international community today. But facing the world's last major Communist-ruled country, Taiwan figures in the West's imagination like a democratic David defying a giant totalitarian Goliath. It is seen as standing on the front line of perhaps the greatest ideological clash of the modern era, where the authoritarian and the liberal democratic worlds come face to face in a struggle for domination that will shape the century in which we live.

All this means that the stakes could not be higher. We live in a world where there is often unease over policies that aim not at resolution and solution but merely at management and deflection. But the stark fact is that the Taiwan–China issue, as of today, has no solution, and is of such momentous importance and danger that no attempt should be made to impose one. Ambiguity and hedging have avoided conflict so far. It may appear paradoxical, but this book will be a passionate defence of why the outside world needs to recommit to ambiguity and hedging with clarity and focus as never before.

Maintaining this position will be a challenge, and will fray some people's nerves. Taiwan is not recognized diplomatically by the vast majority of the world's countries. And yet morally, it is widely supported. During the COVID-19 pandemic, when the Chinese adopted a far more assertive tone in their diplomacy towards Taiwan, countries such as Lithuania clearly illustrated how the status quo is being challenged. In 2021, the Lithuanian government allowed a Taiwanese trade office to be established in the capital, Vilnius, implying greater recognition and engagement than normal. The Lithuanians also spelled out greater support for Taiwan and its struggle with Beijing in a new policy paper. The Chinese government unleashed its fury, recalling its ambassador from Vilnius and downgrading diplomatic representation, stopping 90 per cent of its exports to the Baltic state and launching a volley of fiery rhetoric. The Lithuanians stood firm (their trade with China was limited in any case). Clearly China intended this as an example for others to observe and reflect on: this is what happens to a country that decides to become inventive on Taiwan-related issues and seek stronger links with the island.

While this and other events were sharp reminders to the rest of the world of the difficulty of managing relations with China, Taiwan itself was continuing to cope with these sorts of tensions and problems as a daily reality. Despite the island's dispute with its huge neighbour, China still accounted for almost half its trade and is the home to almost 200,000 of its people. As COVID-19 spread, claims of misinformation about the disease and where fault lay for the crisis sparked off a domestic campaign to increase what Taiwan's Digital Minister Audrey Tang called people's 'information resilience'. Part of the aim of this book is to provide a little more information resilience for those thinking through the Taiwan issue as it inches towards a fatal tipping point, in the hope that we never get there.

1.   *Taiwan Life*

Who are the Taiwanese? What makes them distinctive? These questions lie at the heart of understanding the Taiwan–China challenge today. If Taiwanese all felt they were purely Chinese and part of China, there would be no issue. Reunification would have happened long ago. If this were just a matter of territory and property, then that too could be sorted out, even if with difficulty and argument. But the reality is that the links between Taiwan and China are hard to categorize and capture. These places and their inhabitants cannot be wholly separated, but neither can they be seen as largely the same. The most difficult thing to form a clear judgement on is *how* Taiwan and China are different, and whether whatever similarities they have provide the grounds for linking them more closely.

A very simple way to answer the question 'Who are the Taiwanese?' is to say that they are people who live in a specific place. Taiwan is an island resembling the shape of a diamond, stretched across part of the East China Sea. It has been sundered from the main land mass of China for 4 million years. It exists today, according to the words of Taiwan Digital Minister Audrey Tang, as a result of the 'conflict' when collision between vast pieces of geography in deep history left the island and its many smaller satellites in the shape they are now. It is apt that a place often talked of as sitting at the centre of the greatest geopolitical clash of our age has dramatic conflict encoded in its very geology, and that it is forged from the encounter of ancient, epic forces. The sea between China and

Taiwan is often choppy, sometimes rough even for good quality boats, far from ideal for those who in the past sought to flee to the island, or for those who wanted to escape it. In modern times, those waters have served as a great asset for defence and protection.

To be Taiwanese today, however, is about much more than the specific land on which one lives. History, identity, culture and values are constant issues and questions defining one's daily life. All of these offer rich grounds for argument and disagreement. Take a very simple example, like stating which nationality Taiwanese believe they have. The many citizens of the island who travel today carry a passport like everyone else. It is olive green, a standard, unremarkable document similar to every other country's. But for many years in the 1990s and into the 2000s, there was a fierce argument in Taiwan about which words should go on the cover to identify the nationality of the bearer. 'Republic of China' was the phrase used up to 2020. The People's Republic could tolerate that, even if it didn't like it, because at least it had the all-important word 'China', recognizing a common link. But from the early 2000s, the Taiwanese government tried to replace that name simply with 'Taiwan'.

This was part of the 'Taiwanization' process, an attempt to assert local identity above an overarching Chinese one, promoted by the newly elected Democratic Progressive Party (DPP) president, Chen Shui-bian. Domestically within the island, there were people who vehemently opposed this, because they believed that reunification with what they regarded as their homeland would one day happen. These Taiwanese with stronger feelings and links with the mainland (some of whom had either been born there or were children of people who had been) didn't agree with strong assertions of local identity. They felt this threatened their belief that they were, in the end, Chinese. *Taipei People*, a novel by Pai Hsien-yung published in 1971, captured this kind of linkage beautifully, describing people who, despite more than two decades on the island, still pined for their old homes on the mainland, and were afflicted by nostalgia and vivid memories of where they came from. From the 1950s into the 1980s, people could sensibly say they were Chinese or Taiwanese-Chinese. Many did. For many others, however, particularly the ones with no living memory of China in the way Pai's novel described, 'Republic of China' meant little. 'Taiwan' was where they lived – why couldn't that go on their passport? This is precisely what finally happened in 2020 when a compromise of sorts was at last achieved. Both names were put on the front of the document. But the English for 'Taiwan' was in larger type and more prominent.

Identity, though, is about more than just a name. It is also about recognition and validation from others. Furnished with this document, the Taiwanese citizen will get unfettered visa-free access to more than 140 countries (one of the most user-friendly passports in the world). But the moment they take one of the many hundreds of direct flights from their homeland to China, their passport becomes useless. To gain entry there they instead need to use a separate, special document – a 'Taiwanese compatriot's ID card' – and go along specific immigration channels usually reserved for citizens of China. Whether they like it or not, they will be counted as a local when entering the People's Republic, a traveller who has crossed no national boundaries to make the journey despite all the evidence to the contrary.

For Taiwanese, this sort of experience makes it clear to them that their identity is not straightforward, and that a powerful player existing right next door to them has strong views on who they say they are. Indeed, the way that Taiwanese and Chinese identities are related to each other has become increasingly vexed and complicated over the years since the two became divided and pursued separate paths. It is on the question of how people are permitted to identify themselves that the chief claims made by China ultimately reside, with its insistence that people on both sides of the strait belong to one family, one society, one state. They are first and foremost Chinese, and that takes precedence over whatever else they say they are. Being called Chinese, for Taiwanese, is like summoning up a shadow self, a part of one's identity that is hostage to forces and assertions that are beyond one's control.

More Chinese Than the Chinese?

One complication in all this is that being Chinese culturally has been regarded by many Taiwanese as positive and as something they accept and are often proud of. They believe this quality exists separately from the current iteration of it put out by the People's Republic, as something almost boundary-less and abstract in nature. Coming to the island in early 2024 for the presidential election, I started to reflect on the first time I had visited, almost a quarter of a century earlier. Back then, I was often told by people – both from the island and from China, as well as those outside it – that if I wanted to see 'real Chinese culture' I would need to go to Taiwan. So much of the best material and art from the past, they said, had either been taken there before 1949 or preserved better as the mainland had gone through waves of revolution, destruction and change. Taiwan, I was told, was more Chinese than China.

Plenty of Taiwanese did indeed believe their form of

Chineseness was as valid and authentic as the variant on the mainland, if not more so. A friend in the 2000s told me proudly how the old, traditional-style full-form characters of written Chinese were maintained on the island, despite being replaced by a simpler form of writing in China itself. Then there was family life, and the huge residue of Confucianism and traditional Chinese culture. Taiwan had seen none of the communization, the breaking down of family networks and the attacks on what was labelled the 'old feudal society' that had been China's fate since the 1950s. In the Cultural Revolution from 1966 to 1976, Confucian temples had been destroyed, even in the ancient philosopher's birthplace of Qufu, in the northern part of the People's Republic. While this was happening, Confucianism was still celebrated in Taiwan and taught in schools as a valid ethical system to base one's life on.

In the years since that first visit, I have come to appreciate that the relationship of Taiwanese to Chineseness has become far more complex. So many things have happened over the intervening quarter of a century to change how people on the island feel about themselves. Democracy has developed; society has evolved, like everywhere else. In the 1980s and 1990s, Taiwanese were taught in school that their country still owned not just the whole mainland but Mongolia too, and that their history was the dynastic history of China, a country they were still part of despite its temporary schism since the Civil War. They looked at maps pinned to the walls saying that the Republic they lived in stretched thousands of kilometres to the north, rather than ending in the scatter of islands across a hundred or so kilometres of the seas around them. I am not alone in this observation. 'The Taiwan that China wants,' wrote the BBC's Rupert Wingfield-Hayes during the 2024 election, 'is vanishing.' He went on to say that 'the island's burgeoning identity is once again being tested as Taiwan votes in a new government . . . And with each election, China is more troubled by the assertion of a Taiwanese identity – one that thwarts the chances of what it calls "peaceful reunification" with the mainland.'[1]

It wasn't just the Taiwanese who were changing. The Chinese too were undergoing rapid economic and social transformation. The country was being rebuilt and redeveloped. It was also becoming politically more nationalistic and authoritarian than anyone expected. With every passing day, Taiwanese and Chinese were growing more distinct from each other. The more China was saying to Taiwan how similar they were and what deep bonds held them together, the more Taiwanese were saying they disagreed.

Surveys in the twenty-first century have backed up this sense of a visible and dramatic shift in Taiwanese evaluations of their own identity. A Pew Research Center survey conducted in 2023–4 showed that a mere 3 per cent of those questioned said they felt primarily Chinese; 28 per cent said they felt both Chinese and Taiwanese; and a commanding 67 per cent said they regarded themselves as solely Taiwanese. To the question 'Do you feel emotionally attached to China?' the answer was even starker, with 85 per cent replying in the negative.[2] Polls by the National Chengchi University in Taipei have tracked this shift in public views. Back in 1992, when the first was carried out, 17 per cent said they were Taiwanese, and 25 per cent Chinese, with 46 per cent saying both.[3] The move in public sentiment has been seismic and decisive. In a situation where so many things are ambiguous and often deliberately blurred, this fact is blatantly clear: polls since 2000 have consistently and increasingly shown that however Taiwanese define themselves, being solely Chinese is not one of them.

Taiwan and Pluralism

Instead, Taiwanese people today have a self-identity that is as varied as the landscape in which they live. It is not that Taiwanese aren't influenced by China – but their identity contains a lot more. It has always been a place of porousness, where influences from elsewhere wash over the society and the landscape. The Dutch, Japanese, English, Spanish and many others have left their unwanted mark. So too did many different areas of China itself, along with flows of people far deeper in the past, such as those today who are of aboriginal heritage or from across the wider Asian region. A rich array of people have come over the centuries – merchants, pirates, those fleeing persecution and war elsewhere. Taiwan was often a refuge from the mainland. This was one reason why Chinese imperial rulers in the past were at first so hesitant to try to assimilate it into their empire. They regarded it as a wild, uncivilized place, somewhere beyond the pale, a home for the marginalized and outcasts.

Much of the island today is heavily industrialized. Most of what one can see with the naked eye is the sort of typical developed scene one might see anywhere. The ubiquitous multi-lane highways heaving with lorries, cars, taxis and scooters crisscross the world's second most densely populated region after Bangladesh. Going on the high-speed train south towards Taizhong, a city in the central part of the island, in early 2024, I watched through the window as the same endless generic buildings, factories, warehouses and parking lots that sprawl across the rest of the industrialized world flashed by. The breakneck modernization that occurred during the 1950s and into the 1970s, which made Taiwan celebrated as an economic powerhouse, brought with it the same forces that eroded local distinctiveness elsewhere and created this surface appearance of uniformity. This, rather than anything more deliberate, erased many of the signs of Chinese cultural influence. (Ironically, it did the same in China too, though at a later date, from the 1980s onwards.)

It isn't just modern globalization that has shaped the contemporary Taiwanese sense of a unique identity. For fifty years, from 1895 to the end of the Second World War, the island was a colony of Japan. Memories of this era sneak through, sometimes with unsettling power. A wall preserved in the Da'an area of Taipei carries a plaque testifying to its function as part of the central city prison's perimeter in the first half of the twentieth century, when the Japanese were in charge. Dissidents and opponents of the regime, and then American soldiers, were incarcerated here. But even in places like this, the trauma they might stir up has been subsequently ameliorated. Remnants of the walls of the old, distinctively Japanese-style buildings serve as a cultural centre, and as a place for bars, workshops and small eateries – an oasis of calmness and peace amidst relics of the past.

Japan is present in various other places across the island. In the mountains around Taipei, there are beautiful retreats and spas which remind you of the hot springs so common in Japan. So too can the restaurants serving fresh fish in the Japanese style, many of them as good as anything Tokyo or Kyoto can offer. Japanese signage is everywhere, and the Japanese have become increasingly important visitors since 2016 and the fall-off in Chinese tourists, when poor cross-strait relations caused the Beijing government to ban individual travellers and only allow designated groups to go to the island. In 2016, 1.9 million Japanese came to Taiwan. The feelings of attraction were reciprocated: 4.17 million, almost a fifth of Taiwan's population, went to Japan that same year. This same group of Japanese visitors was also the largest-spending tourist cohort.[4]

Taiwan Values

Chinese, Japanese and generic global modernity are the great forces inscribed on Taiwan's landscape today. But it is in the intangible area of values and beliefs that differences are found. Despite a common cultural root in many areas, Taiwanese and Chinese are different because of the very different values they have come to embrace. Civic society in the People's Republic was never fully accepted, even in the more liberal 1990s and 2000s. Now every organization and entity in China has to have links to the all-powerful Communist Party, which governs everything. Taiwan is the opposite: a place which has come to value diversity and pluralism. It was the first Asian country to legalize same-sex marriages in 2019. Civic society has grown stronger as the democratization process begun in the 1990s has thrived. By 2022, according to one report, 'there were 127 political associations (including political parties); 11,324 occupational associations; and 61,863 social associations, including 21,974 national associations and 39,889 local associations'.[5] Unlike China, there are no restrictions on who can set up groups, and what areas they can cover or what their operations entail, as long as they operate within the law.

Pluralism also applies to religious belief – and the freedom to worship as people choose, something that is definitely not the case on the mainland, where tight controls are exercised. Taiwanese values come from the different religions practised on the island. In a survey in 2021, 28 per cent of the population said they subscribed to traditional folk religions, 20 per cent identified as Buddhist, and 19 per cent as Daoist, while 24 per cent said they were nonbelievers. For the rest of the country, the balance is made up of Christians (Protestants represent 5.5 per cent and Catholics 1.4 per cent). There are also smaller communities of Jews (two synagogues) and Sunni Muslims (eleven mosques). Added to the mix are followers of the Heaven Emperor Religion, the Heaven Virtue Religion, the Yellow Emperor Religion, the Church of Scientology, the Baha'i Faith, Jehovah's Witnesses, the Church of Jesus Christ of Latter-day Saints, and the Unification Church.[6] Whatever else the island might be, one thing is indisputable: it is a place of huge variety in terms of what people believe and the Gods they worship.

That hybridity between Chinese tradition and Western modernity was there from early on in the establishment of the Republic of China on Taiwan. Chiang Kai-shek, the founder of the country in its current guise, exemplified this as a man who was as much a Christian as a Confucianist. The guiding ideology of the Nationalist Party that he led, and which dominated the politics of the island from the late 1940s to the 1990s, was the creed of Sun Yatsen. His memorial sits grandly at the centre of Taipei, where he is revered as the founder of modern Chinese nationalism, despite being president of the newly founded Republic for only a few weeks in 1912. But his three 'principles of the people' – democracy, nationalism and people's livelihood – which figure partly in the national education system today, spell out a broader vision of Chinese identity where different faiths, world views and visions can be embraced. Ironically, in the twenty-first century Taiwan holds to these principles and practises them more than China does, even though the People's Republic presents itself as the great bastion and defender of true Chinese identity.

There are also the spiritual beliefs of Taiwan's aboriginal peoples, who presently constitute about 5 per cent of the island's total population. Their culture is visible in protected sacred places such as the hauntingly beautiful Sun Moon Lake, where a small island formation at the centre of the water lies off limits to the boats sailing around it, because of its significance to the local communities whose life here reaches back tens of thousands of years.

Whatever the role of religion in people's lives, what sits at the heart of it all is a sense of humaneness. Here there are overlaps with at least some strands of Chinese cultural and intellectual tradition. Family and extended family networks, despite all the impact is of globalization, continue to matter enormously. The Confucian hierarchy with its five main relationships (ruler and subject, father and son, elder brother and younger brother, husband and wife, and friend and friend), while patriarchal and conservative, has had a profound impact on society to this day. In view of Confucianism's stress on caring for and respecting the elderly, looking after a wide family network, and being obedient to rulers and administrators who act like parental figures, it is unsurprising that Taiwan today has a strong civil society. Confucianism supports the idea of society as a sturdy network, with bonds of responsibility between different people. This manifests itself now in strong social welfare systems, and some of the best hospitals and healthcare in the world.

This notion of social responsibility and the importance of caring for others was very evident during the COVID-19 pandemic. Taiwan never imposed the sort of state-mandated national lockdowns that India, the UK, many countries in Europe, and parts of the US and China had. Nor were people ordered to wear masks or maintain social distancing.

Throughout the crisis, people travelled, carried on working and going to school or university, and government offices and companies stayed open. What was different was the immediate and widespread voluntary compliance with mask-wearing, testing for the virus, and self-isolation for those infected. That meant that, by 2023, Taiwan had relatively low infection rates and mortality rates under the global average in proportion to its population, with 19,000 deaths and 10 million infections.[7] Its success at combatting the virus with limited social impact was held up as a model for others. Much of this achievement was down to the cooperative ethos amongst the Taiwanese population.

This is not to claim that Taiwan is a paradise, a place where the nuclear family unit is inviolable, and everyone looks after everyone else. There are the same rising levels of divorce and single-parent households as in other developed societies.[8] Nor is it a harmonious utopia free of crime. In the past, the mafia ran parts of the island so effectively they kidnapped people from wealthy families and demanded ransoms at will. As late as 2005, gangster boss Chang His-ming was finally apprehended after he and his group were involved in kidnapping ten people.[9] And while, on the whole, crime rates are amongst the lowest in the world, violent crime is not unknown.

The source of strength for a community can be the basis for its flaws as well. Taiwanese are deeply networked with their families and friends, but that can also mean they are insular and prejudicial. In the period since the 1990s, when the national birth rate slowed down and it became harder to find workers to fill positions within Taiwan, Southeast Asian migrants have come to the island in reasonable numbers to take up those jobs that needed to be filled. In spite of Taiwan's ostensible diversity, many have experienced prejudice and unfair practices against them, with South Asian resident workers complaining in 2023 of extra checks at immigration when returning to the island after visits home to their families, and Indian people worried by a rise in online hate speech in Taiwan the same year.[10] To be Taiwanese today, therefore, is to be tolerant in terms of values, lifestyle and political or cultural beliefs. But there is a big question mark over just how far this toleration extends.

Being Taiwanese and the Challenge of Normal

When trying to understand what governs life in Taiwan today, normality is not high on the list. Beyond the abnormality of how most of the outside world treats the island as a state but refuses to recognize it formally as one, there is also the persistent underlying sense of crisis and unease in the Taiwanese own environment. That their huge neighbour to the north has such a strong view on how the Taiwanese should see themselves – and has said it will use force to react if the island errs too much in saying things about itself it doesn't agree with – has an obvious impact. To say you are American or British carries zero danger most of the time. To say you are Taiwanese, and imply that Taiwan is an independent sovereign state, is a far riskier statement, particularly if there are people from China around you.

One of the unnerving things about visiting Taiwan today is seeing the ways in which normality prevails despite this underlying sense of crisis and instability. That other great holdover from the Cold War era, the division between North and South Korea, is a good example of a conflict also placed into deep freeze in the early post-Second World War period. Both North and South Korea, and China and Taiwan, are situations where each party claims sovereignty over the other (though in the case of Taiwan in recent years, that stance has changed, with many wanting straight independence for their island, and having no interest in claims over the mainland). Both involve a liberal, capitalist partner on one side, and an authoritarian, Communist-run system on the other. Both pose major security challenges for the region and for the globe, and neither looks close to resolution.

But in terms of the situation on the ground, North and South Korea and Taiwan and China are worlds apart. The Chinese version of one-party rule works in a system with large elements of dynamic capitalism, unlike North Korea, where state control over the economy is almost complete. And with its nuclear programme and frequent launching of missiles into the seas around it, North Korea is far more overtly bellicose than China (the firing of a powerful, long-range intercontinental ballistic missile in July 2023 was followed by another demonstration of North Korean ballistic technology in December, provoking the condemnation of the G7).[11]

The calmness and normality prevailing in Taiwan might tempt observers into thinking that its conflict with China is not as pressing or urgent as that between North and South Korea. Arriving on the island reinforces this unnerving sense of humdrum mundanity. There are no obvious signs at the airport near Taipei of imminent attack or heightened need for security. Heading into the city, it is as rare to see military personnel (unlike in North Korea, where the army is everywhere). People get on with their lives, doing what they would do even if there was no looming threat over their heads. It is only on the islands close to the PRC coast that there are tangible signs of tension, with clashes between fishing vessels near Jinmin island in

February 2024 (during which two Chinese fishermen drowned). But even here, as one report stated, 'it's life as usual . . . Residents go about their business on quiet streets shrouded in fog and rain.'[12]

Despite the semblance of normality, there are worrying signs of the deeper reality. A few days after my arrival in early 2024, an emergency message rang out on my smartphone while I was in the lift returning to my hotel room. 'Air raid alert,' it said. 'Missile flyover Taiwan airspace. Be aware.' It made me think of how rare it was to see any real evidence that Taiwan was indeed 'the world's most dangerous place', as *The Economist* proclaimed in 2021.[13] But a quick look at the statistics the local Ministry of Defence produces on Chinese military aircraft trespassing into Taiwanese airspace was a sobering reminder of this danger. In 2022 alone, 1,727 Chinese planes from the People's Liberation Army Air Force were recorded entering Taiwan's air defence zone, almost double the year before, and a huge increase over the 381 incidents in 2020.[14] There was also the case of the ballistic missiles China launched over the island into the seas beyond during the visit of Nancy Pelosi, then Speaker of the US House of Representatives, in August 2022. These were enough to force international flights to Taipei to be redirected or postponed.

Accordingly, there are small signboards on almost every street of air raid bunkers. Beyond that, an insistent calmness prevails. Even the warning message my smartphone received about the missile flyovers stoked suspicions in the local press of a more political motive. One representative of the Nationalist Party wondered if it was to stir up a sense of threat that would strengthen the ruling DPP and its tougher stance towards the mainland during the election season.[15] When I spoke to the owner of a shop where I went to buy some fruit a few hours after the message came through, they downplayed what had just happened as the government pumping out over-cautious messaging. Their relaxed attitude both impressed and worried me, because I wasn't as confident as them that having ballistic missiles tossed into your airspace, even if they weren't aimed at anything in particular, was something to be so quickly dismissed. Such is contemporary life on the island.[16]

Indeed, for many Taiwanese, the more imminent threat is a natural one from their own weather and geography, rather than the human one from their neighbour. In 2023, temperatures almost touching forty degrees centigrade were recorded for several days. People had to hold umbrellas over their heads to shelter as they walked under the relentless sun. The typhoons that hit the coasts of the main island most years made sure this one was no exception in terms of extreme weather. In October, Typhoon Koinu reached land with wind speeds of more than 200 kilometres an hour in the southern part of the country.[17] A month earlier, Typhoon Haikui had skirted the island, turning back on its route to brush its coasts, before heading towards the mainland.[18] Global warming is a real and live issue in a place at the heart of the modern industrial revolution. In Taipei, the hottest day ever was recorded on 24 July 2020, when thermometers reached a sweltering 39.7 degrees.[19] As an official statement from the Taiwanese Ministry of Foreign Affairs declared in 2018, 'The increasing frequency of extreme weather events and rising sea levels caused by global warming endanger Taiwan's environment and survival.'[20]

Matters are not helped by the previously mentioned great tectonic fault lines that the island sits on, which mean that over the last century there have been earthquakes almost every year. Their impact has often been deadly. One earthquake about 150 kilometres south of Taipei in 1999 reached 7.7 on the

Richter scale, killing more than 2,000 people and destroying 10,000 houses.[21] In November 2023, a movement out at sea caused the buildings in Taipei to tremble. In April 2024, the strongest earthquake in a quarter of a century killed nine people and destroyed numerous buildings and roads. When it is not blasts of wind, or satellites from China causing anxiety from the sky, it is turmoil from underground. Part of Taiwanese identity these days is to deal with these things and not make a fuss. That is what constitutes 'normal' in the Taiwan of today.

2. How It Started, How It's Going: Taiwan's History

Since the time of the ancient Greek Herodotus, often described as the Father of History, storytellers have been the narrators of history, discerning patterns, identifying underlying trends, making sense of what has happened. The Taiwan story is a particularly rich one, a gift for such weavers of tales. Woven into it are intermittent war, rebellion and the fight for freedom and autonomy, as well as the actors who have played a role, from the waves of migration to the travellers and pirates and seekers of trading opportunities who have come to make their lives on the island. It is in this profuse, varied, complex story reaching back thousands of years that better sense can be made of Taiwanese identity today, and of how the influences of China – and other places – have knitted themselves into the narrative of the island and its people.

The great National Palace Museum in Taipei, located in the outskirts of the capital, is recognized as the most extensive and highest quality collection of Chinese imperial treasures in the world. It is a monument to the splendour and diversity of the history of the Chinese world. But even the most cursory visit would establish that it is an assemblage of masterworks that originate not from the island but from the vast historic territory of the many Chinas that have existed over the last three millennia. Its presence in the purpose-designed buildings that cling to its hillside setting today was the result of the accident and chaos of the Sino-Japanese War of the 1930s and 1940s. It therefore stands as much a memorial to this more recent history as it does to the distant past.

First there is the dramatic story of *how* this collection came to end up here. During the Republic of China's fragmentation in the 1920s and 1930s, accelerated by the aggression of the Japanese, a remarkable group of curators and historians in the palace complex of the Forbidden City in Beijing started to worry about what would happen to the collection if the capital were invaded. As the situation deteriorated in the early 1930s, they took the radical decision to move as much as they could to safer parts of the country. Tens of thousands of ancient scrolls, paintings, pottery, ceramics and other priceless artefacts were crated up. First they were carried in convoys of old trucks and on horseback to central China, often in imminent peril from bombing by planes overhead and from soldiers fighting around them on the ground. When matters there worsened, they were taken to Chongqing in the southwest of the country, which served as the capital of the Nationalist-controlled territory, where they were stored while the war was waged against the Japanese.

But return to Beijing – or to any other potential capital of the newly liberated and unified country in 1945 – never happened. The Civil War ended the all too brief interlude of stability in 1946; and with their defeat in 1949, the Nationalists loaded the almost 40,000 wooden crates containing carefully packed artefacts on to ships, some of them rickety and barely seaworthy. One accident, one aberrant wave, one enemy bomb, and some of the greatest creations humanity has ever produced could have sunk to the bottom of the ocean. But miraculously, more than a decade after they first embarked on their long journey, they reached its end in the new capital of the regime, Taipei.[1]

Today, these great treasures of the past betray none of the

trauma of their recent history. They sit in placid peacefulness, either in secure storage, or in purpose-made display cases where hundreds of thousands of visitors each year can marvel at them. One of the highlights is the bronze cauldron (or ding) of Duke Mao, a tangible reminder of the sheer longevity of Chinese civilization; the 500 characters written on it almost 3,000 years ago are still legible to most Chinese speakers today (these register the appointment of the duke). The most famous exhibits, however, are two small objects. Both, tellingly, given the importance of food culture on the island, involve the representation of edible things. The first is a cabbage with an impossibly delicate grasshopper perched on it. The carving is made of pure jade, regarded by ancient Chinese as the most precious of all stones due to its association with longevity. Some call this tiny sculpture the 'Mona Lisa of the East'. The second is a gemstone which has been worked to give it the colouration and contours of a piece of cooked pork. Surrounding the cases that protect these works of art are usually crowds of tourists several rows deep.

Yet the vast majority of the museum's holdings are from a time when Taiwan did not even figure in the Chinese world. They are from another place and another time. The National Palace Collection raises a number of questions. What is the nature of Chineseness, and how singular and binding is it? Are the artefacts here expressions of a common, stable and unified tradition – one to which the people in Taiwan today belong, just as much as the people on the mainland?

The History of the Earliest Taiwanese

Only a little distance from the National Palace Museum, there is a far less visited collection. The Shung Ye Museum of Formosan

Aborigines recounts the other history of the island: the far older story of communities from diverse places, speaking a variety of dialects and languages, practising their own distinct rites, who lived in this place for tens of thousands of years. For these people, Chinese culture was alien, and belonged to outsiders. For at least 5 per cent of the Taiwanese population today, this history is part of their ethnic heritage, and increasingly a thread of the national narrative that speaks of the island's uniqueness and integrity as a place that should be understood in its own right.

Taiwan was colonized much as Australia and America were, albeit by people from China rather than Europe. As in Australia and America, the signs of the earliest native communities are now faint and must be searched for. The first inhabitants of Taiwan were of Austronesian ancestry. Ethnologists today still argue over whether they were of Indonesian origin from the south, or if significant groups migrated from the north, through China.[2]

Whatever their origin, those first communities settled on the main island of Taiwan from 20,000 to 6,000 years ago, and hunted and farmed its land before they were exposed over the last millennium to an almost continuous flow of immigration by people from across the strait. This was not a structured or deliberate process. Taiwan existed at the outer edge of Chinese consciousness.[3] One of the island's earliest mentions in Chinese sources occurred 1,800 years ago, when the emperor Sun Chuan of the Three Kingdoms Dynasty despatched an expedition to explore the islands off the coast of the empire in 230 CE.[4] After this single reference, Taiwan barely figured in the rich archive of Chinese-language material for centuries. It cropped up again in 1349, during the time of the Yuan Dynasty, when the explorer Wang Dayuan provided the first written account of the island by a Chinese visitor. But the attention of the dynasty's Mongol rulers soon passed from this little land off the coast of their immense realm as they struggled to maintain their grip on power.[5]

Initially, only a tiny number of Chinese settlers chanced fate and made the crossing from the mainland coast. They were usually amongst the most impoverished people in society. In the words of one of the most celebrated historians of modern Taiwan, Su Beng, they were 'the Han serfs' who 'opened Taiwan at the price of their own toil, their own sweat, their own blood'.[6] Many were fleeing poverty or conflict back home in China. These, coming in waves over many generations, constitute the ancestry of the majority of Taiwanese today.

Early Chinese merchants had frequently complained of the native people's aggression towards voyagers who landed on the island for provisions. But the indigenous population was unable to repel the stream of colonists; over the decades, it was gradually corralled within the island's hinterland. From the sixteenth century, Chinese and English sources referred to the indigenous peoples as 'mountain tribes'. However, beginning in the 1620s, settlers who came to the island increasingly found that most of the inhabitable territory was controlled not by the native population but by Dutch and Spanish nationals. Merchants of these two great competing sea powers were exploiting trading opportunities in the region, creating the first vestiges of modern global supply chains, shifting goods from Asia back to markets in Europe. Their main bases were in today's Indonesia for the Dutch, and the Philippines for the Spanish. But the source of so much of what they wanted in the seventeenth century – from silk and spices, to tea and porcelain – was not there, but in the great empire of China. And beyond the small entrepôt of Macau, ceded on indeterminate leases to the

Portuguese in the middle of the sixteenth century, the rest of the country was off limits to foreigners. Opportunities for trading were tantalizing, but a fraction of what they could have acquired with greater access.

Taiwan offered a handy landing ground, close to the potential source of great enrichment on the Chinese mainland, but safely not part of it. The Dutch, who had succeeded by the 1630s in squeezing the Spanish out and gaining control of part of the island for themselves, buttressed their influence by building permanent fortresses and houses. In view of the efforts they made to establish trading posts and send people to settle, they intended to stay for good. This 'Ilha Formosa' ('Beautiful Island' in Portuguese), as they called Taiwan, became part of their great trade network. The remnants of that time are now faint traces on the modern landscape. Fort Zeelandia, in today's Tainan in central Taiwan, is the most dramatic, its imposing walls still standing four centuries after they were built. It was from here that the Dutch East India Company, under instructions from its headquarters in Batavia (today's Jakarta), set out to finally develop trade in China. This was to be the launching pad for the most coveted market in the world.

But for all these aspirations and plans of Europeans, other change was afoot. The empire ruled from Beijing was undergoing significant upheaval. Northern tribes, the Manchus, usurped the rule of the Ming Dynasty in the 1640s, inaugurating a new regime, the Bright – or 'Qing' – Dynasty. This was to be one of the most acquisitive and ambitious dynasties in Chinese imperial history. Armies were sent to pacify the territories along the western borders, bringing what are today Xinjiang and Tibet into the embrace of the new empire. It was only a matter of time before the southern coast's security became an issue and Taiwan, for the first time, was drawn more tightly into China's orbit.

Becoming Part of China – After a Fashion

What caught the attention of the new Manchu rulers was not the Dutch presence on Taiwan. It was the loyalist bandits, supporters of the old regime, who had fled there from their initial holdout in Fujian and along the southern coast of the country the Manchus now ruled. In a striking parallel to the situation in the twentieth century, the mainland leaders saw Taiwan as a centre for rebels, groups faithful to the old order fighting to see its restoration. Most of these rebels were of the dominant Han ethnicity rather than Manchus, giving their defiance an extra level of significance. They even established a parallel Tungning Dynasty, which was centred on the island but had claims to the rest of the empire.

The leader of these rebels, Zheng Chenggong (or 'Koxinga', as he is often called in literature of the time) was a figure who inspired devotion and fascination amongst his followers, and intense levels of fury from China's new rulers. He was a man of mixed parentage: his mother came from Japan; his Chinese father had originally joined the rebellion but ultimately turned and went over to the Qing. Zheng did not emulate his father's compromise: he undertook a spirited insurgency, waging war and wreaking havoc on the mainland till all of his forces were compelled to flee across the strait to Taiwan in 1661. As with Chiang Kai-shek's flight to the island in the late 1940s, Zheng claimed his regime on Taiwan was the legitimate government of the empire. He was the ultimate romantic rebel, someone granted almost godlike status by those under him. As for the

Dutch, they were expelled in the same violent way they had evicted the Spanish, finally forced out by Zheng's armies in 1662. But the victorious rebel leader had little time to enjoy his success, dying only a few months later. His son, Zheng Jing, took over his mantle, and for twenty years managed to make the parallel empire survive on the island.

Small, populated by rebels and people living beyond the law, who were harried as much by the indigenous local people who wanted to drive them out as by the Qing Chinese who wanted to destroy them – Taiwan in the mid-seventeenth century was no tropical paradise. But the great Kangxi emperor, who ascended to the imperial throne in 1661 aged only six and reigned for more than sixty years, made the fateful decision that this territory on the fringes of his realm should belong to the Qing empire. This was driven by larger geopolitical considerations regarding the defence of China's territory. Acquisition of the island was not about gaining land per se; Kangxi dismissed the real estate he was demanding his armies conquer as merely a 'mud ball in the sea'. What was important was security. It was simply inadmissible to have the coastal districts of the southern Qing empire vulnerable to attack by Zheng dissidents and rebels.

As with the contemporaneous conquests of Xinjiang and then Tibet launched by Kangxi, the priority was to create a zone of safety around his regime's heartland. Taiwan was like a small dagger pointed threateningly at the throat of China. The emperor issued an edict commanding the pacification of this rebellious place; a full-scale invasion occurred in 1683, and complete annexation a year later. The final Zheng ruler, Keshuang, was taken to Beijing, where he saw out his days as a loyal subject of the regime. After discussion amongst officials at the imperial court about whether or not to simply ship all the current inhabitants back to the mainland and abandon the island, Taiwan was made a prefecture of the neighbouring province of Fujian. Its inhabitants were allowed to stay.

An official from the southern part of China, Yu Yonghe, offers a vivid first-hand account of these early days after the Zheng regime was defeated by the Qing. He made the treacherous journey across the strait in 1696. His writing about that experience gives a flavour of what the place was like to the urbane eyes of the governing literati on the mainland, a little over a decade after its pacification and acceptance into Qing lands. While noting that the indigenous peoples were 'quite advanced culturally', after a few weeks travelling around the island he complained: 'To live here it is hard enough not to get sick and die, no less to avoid the ghosts stalking you.'[7] Yu's impressions were not improved by his fulfilling his own prediction and falling ill soon after writing down these words. His sigh of relief on leaving at the end of his tour of duty is almost audible across the centuries.

For more than 200 years, Taiwan continued to suffer marginal status. Its reputation amongst outsiders as a place on the edge of the known world, somewhere that typified the outer territory beyond which the influence of Chinese civilization faded and barbarism reigned, remained unchanged. Sporadically, waves of settlers continued to come. Most belonged to two Han peoples from the southern provinces of China closest to Taiwan: the Hakka – whose name means 'guest people' in Cantonese – were mainly from Guangdong and Guangxi; the Hokkien from Fujian. They eked out a living trading what they could, exporting the island's raw materials, such as rice, sugar and deerskin, to the mainland.

The British had been trading intermittently with Taiwan since the 1670s. But in the early eighteenth century, merchants from the British East India Company – established in 1600 in London to pursue a monopoly of commerce with what is now South and East Asia – gained a foothold on the island, as did some of the private traders increasingly involved in the opium business then developing from its source in India. They worked around the burdensome restrictions placed on direct trade with the mainland by the authorities there, exploiting the more freewheeling remoteness of Taiwan, where the rules were laxly applied. But outsiders still wrote of the inhospitality of the island's residents, the ease of falling sick from malaria, infections, insect bites – and the generally uncomfortable, muggy climate. The weather was impossibly humid, often boiling hot in the summer and prone to devastating typhoons, which ripped up buildings and trees and drenched the land with torrential rain.

On top of that, the island was also a place of almost perpetual rebellion. Some writing at the time quipped that they happened every five years, like clockwork, forcing constant costly intervention from the Qing forces on the mainland. A particularly extensive uprising in 1721 was led by more recent Han settlers, fed up with their hard lot and demanding more support from the Qing authorities. A second revolt flared up a decade later, when indigenous peoples protested against their oppression at the hands of the new settlers and the administration. These events were a stark reminder that Taiwan was somewhere with a divided and antagonistic population. Even by the middle of the nineteenth century, when the British were fresh from their victories in the First and Second Anglo-Chinese Wars of 1839–60 and furnished with the right to open treaty ports across the country, they regarded their outposts on Taiwan as particularly hard places for officials to serve.

It was accident rather than design that brought about

Taiwan's increased prominence in the Chinese imagination. This was the era of the infamous 'scramble for China', when European powers – Britain, Germany, Russia, France and even Italy – bullishly promoted their own commercial interests against those of the fatally weak central government in Beijing. The French were particularly aggressive in Taiwan, demanding to administer the island as a colony (much as Britain would run Hong Kong after a brief war with the Chinese in 1885). Despite the French resorting to military force in 1884–5, their attempt to peel the island away from China was successfully rebuffed; other colonial powers refused to support France's claim, worried that it would give the French too great an advantage. In an effort to bolster Qing authority and reinforce Taiwan's place in the empire, the island was finally raised to the status of a province in 1887, after more than two centuries as a prefecture subordinate to Fujian on the mainland. It was given its own governor and permitted at least some autonomy over its own affairs. But Taiwan's position occupying key trade routes made it too rich a prize for foreign powers not to continue to strive for control of the island ahead of their competitors.

The Japan Years

Within a few years, however, the Japanese were to make an even more forceful move on Taiwan. Their defeat of the Chinese in the Sino-Japanese War of 1894–5 meant they could demand huge indemnities, which included massive financial and territorial concessions. The Treaty of Shimonoseki in 1895 saw Taiwan traded away like a simple commodity, its citizens granted no say in the matter, exchanging their status in the space of a single day from citizens of one empire to another. This was to be their fate for the next half-century. The same treaty also saw the Korean peninsula handed over from Chinese to Japanese control.

Japanese colonization had a profound impact on Taiwan in the first half of the twentieth century and, as noted in the first chapter, has etched marks on the landscape, society and local culture that endure to this day. For those who were born or grew up after 1895, it was likely that they were either bilingual in Chinese and Japanese, or that Japanese was their first language. As the period under the colonizers continued, Japan imposed increasingly stringent cultural demands, mandating that people only speak Japanese, and that Japanese-style clothing must be worn. But the Japanese also built infrastructure in their new possession and worked on the economic development of their new colony. While the Qing regime fragmented and collapsed in 1911, ushering in a period of chaos and economic turbulence across the strait, Taiwan was shielded from this, drawing ahead materially. Taiwanese grew better educated and enjoyed more prosperous lives than their former compatriots on the mainland. But while the locals shared in at least some of the fruits of rapid modernization and industrialization the Japanese were spearheading, they had no say in the governance of their homeland, and largely lived voiceless and marginalized lives.

The Japanese, even when they changed their military governors to civilian ones and finally allowed some kind of elections in the 1930s, were not benign rulers. Despite this, Taiwan was spared the widespread, sustained brutal ravages visited on the mainland during the 1937–45 Sino-Japanese War, though attempts to eradicate indigenous peoples reached almost genocidal levels in the 1930s before being scaled back due to the preoccupation of the Imperial Japanese Army with its conflict on the other side of the strait. This is something dramatically remembered in Wu He's 1999 novel, *Remains of Life*, a harrowing account of the reprisals against the indigenous Atayal Taiwanese in 1930 after they attacked and killed more than 130 Japanese in a remote school in the mountains. The Japanese used poison gas, aerial bombing, and a ground attack by 3,000 of their troops, seeking to eradicate the group. Violence was also deployed against those who agitated for Chinese nationalism – a new force sweeping the rest of the old country – with accused supporters either summarily executed or thrown into jail for lengthy prison terms.

After all this, 1945 and the final defeat of the Japanese in the Second World War were a liberation of sorts. But just like half a century before, Taiwanese still had no voice in their own fate. Their retrocession to the Republic of China was the result not of their own will but of decisions made by the American, British and Soviet Allied powers at summits held in Cairo in 1943 and Potsdam in 1945. It was here that the post-war order was decided. The three main powers (with Chiang Kai-shek present at Cairo, but not at Potsdam) simply agreed that all territory Japan had taken in China would be returned to the Chinese government. There was no definition of what precisely this 'China' was, nor any discussion whether Taiwan might not be a part of it. As an example of excluding those affected by decisions from the actual process of decision-making itself, it was unparalleled.

The situation was compounded by the San Francisco Treaty in 1951, which dealt with the final issues arising from Japan's defeat in 1945. Along with renouncing all claims over various islands, Korea and other Chinese territories, the Japanese government also gave up any rights to the sovereignty of Taiwan.

Confusingly, however – and just like the Cairo Declaration of 1943 and its reaffirmation at Potsdam in 1945 – the treaty did not spell out to whom it was ceding these rights. The existence of two competing entities claiming they were the legitimate government of China meant that neither of the directly affected parties was allowed to attend, as no one knew whom best to invite. Not the least of the confusions this treaty created concerns the Senkaku islands, also known as the Diaoyutai islands, which are today subject to claims by the Republic of China on Taiwan, supported by the People's Republic, against the Japanese.

Brief Encounter: Return to China, 1945–1949

In the 130 years since 1895, Taiwan island only formed part of a unified China for a little over four of them. In that brief period, between 1945 and 1949, it existed as a province, ruled over by a governor of the larger republic. Despite the island's citizens having had no say at all in the decision, the impact of the 1945 return to Chinese rule was huge. The new masters from the Nationalist Party that dominated the mainland were as alien to Taiwanese as the Japanese had been. One American witness at the time, Gordon Kerr, observed a group of natives look on with disdain as one of the mainland soldiers sent to serve on the island pillaged a bicycle from a local. He proved so clueless about such 'modern' technology that, after trying to work out how the mechanism functioned by leaping on it and promptly falling off, he chucked the vehicle away and fled.[8]

These new Chinese arrivals from the mainland, most of them army personnel, claimed to descend from a shared ethnic root with their new fellow island inhabitants. But they were

43

seen as crude, ill-educated, greedy and hailing from an impoverished homeland that had little to do with Taiwan. Most of
these exiles, as one study of the period records, 'were ordinary
folks: common soldiers, petty civil servants, and dispossessed
war refugees from different walks of life'.[9] Many had what was
later called 'sojourner' or 'guest mentality', hoping they would
return where they came from.[10]

The 28 February Incident in 1947 marked the start of what
was subsequently called by historians the time of the 'White
Terror'. Emergency rule was imposed, dissidents harshly pun-
ished and draconian political and media controls exercised – the
objective being to secure the dominance of the Nationalists
under Chiang Kai-shek. On 28 February, rough treatment
against a street vendor accused of selling contraband cigarettes
by officials from the Tobacco Monopoly Bureau provoked protests by onlookers in sympathy with the pedlar. These escalated
until the officials opened fire and one participant in the riot
was killed. Chen Yi, the Chinese governor of the island, initially promised that the government would consider the
protestors' grievances and introduce reforms. But once some
sort of calm had descended, Chiang's armies came in, quelling
the remaining disturbances, which had spread across the island,
in such a brutal manner that it left a dark shadow over the decades that followed. The '228 Event', as it is remembered today,
figured as the moment when Taiwanese truly knew they were
under subjugation from the mainland.

Their situation was to deteriorate markedly as even more
Nationalist forces, failing in the Civil War against the Communists on the mainland, started to seek refuge on the island. By
1949, it is estimated the existing 7 million people in Taiwan had
swelled by a further 2 million mainlanders, most of them arriving by boats from the coast of China. The final defeat of the

Nationalists in 1949 meant that the central government of the Republic of China found itself in exile. Its main leader, Chiang Kai-shek, settled in Taipei, from where he tried to reassemble his forces and plot some means of returning to power on the mainland.

This intense period of migration over the late 1940s into the 1950s brought about profound changes in Taiwan. The presence of so many incomers in such a short period placed serious economic and social burdens on their new home. It created almost overnight a new division in Taiwanese society between the 'local people' and the 'mainlanders'. Inscribed over the existing divisions between people of indigenous and Chinese heritage, this new influx created a cultural clash that continued until the 2000s.

Up to the early 1960s, the situation on the island was constantly precarious. At the very start of the 1950s, the Communists almost settled things in their favour. Their forces were massed on the coast opposite, ready to launch a final full-scale assault. Their dream of a reunified nation seemed about to be realized. Even the Americans, until then increasingly reluctant allies of the Nationalists, were resigned to seeing their former partners succumb to defeat. US President Harry Truman, with a healthy disdain for Chiang and his corrupt, inefficient rule, expected Mao Zedong's army to finish the Civil War in the Communists' favour.

It was not to be. This was not because of any fiendishly clever countermove by Chiang, or lack of will by Mao. Instead, the continued existence of a separate Taiwan was mostly due to events in Korea. At the end of the Second World War, the peninsula had been divided between two separate political entities. The decision of the North Korean leader Kim Il Sung in June 1950, apparently sanctioned by Joseph Stalin in Moscow, to launch a full-scale attack in a bid to reunify with the South caused the United States, via the United Nations, to intervene. The UN's aim was to prevent a major part of Asia (the whole of the Korean peninsula) falling largely under Communist rule. The Chinese were forced to redeploy millions of their troops in defence of their fellow Communist neighbour after the Allied forces managed first to repel the North Korean army and then to push it almost to the Chinese border. Mao's own son Anying died in the subsequent fighting. The attack on Taiwan, so imminent and so close, was called off at the last minute.

While the 1950s saw two crises in the strait, when missiles were fired and the outer islands of Kinmen (often also called Jinmin or Quemoy) and Matsu were shelled by mainland forces, the Korean War reinforced America's commitment to being a constant presence in the region, bringing the Cold War deep into Asia. A mutual defence pact between Washington and the Nationalists in Taipei, signed in 1954, secured Taiwan's immediate future, with both parties pledging to maintain their capacity – separately and collectively – to, in the words of the treaty, 'resist armed attack and Communist subversive activities directed from without against their territorial integrity and political stability'.[11] Any attack on either of them would be met with a unified US–Taiwan response. This marked the point when the security interests of the two became deeply entwined with each other. And though the treaty was voided in 1979, when Washington shifted its formal diplomatic recognition to Beijing, the spirit of alliance spelled out in 1954 remains alive today, even if the terms have changed.

The reckless adventurism of one man, Kim Il Sung, set up the divide between Taiwan and China by causing the distraction and redeployment of China's forces so that the mainland was unable to launch its final invasion of the island. But it was the stubbornness of two others that set this situation in stone. Chiang Kai-shek and Mao Zedong may have differed greatly in ideological outlook, but in terms of intransigence and inflexibility there was very little to tell them apart. Just as Mao brooked no compromise in his belief of the need for a great, unified country under Communist rule, which one day Taiwan would be part of, so Chiang remained adamant until he died in 1975 that the mainland would be retaken and Nationalist government restored. The cleaving of the country was in many ways the result of two ageing men's longstanding feud.

The North Koreans had saved Taiwan by their surprise move in 1950. They had also internationalized the issue of cross-strait relations. Now, more than ever before, a third party was present in the dispute: the United States. The island had been marginal for much of its history, treated as a place to be traded and ceded on the edges of the Chinese empire; from the Korean War, however, the Taiwan issue became not just about the two contending parties, but about the confrontation between fundamentally different views of the world order. Taiwan now sat between the fiercely competitive opposing systems and outlooks represented by Washington and Beijing. That transformed its domestic politics and everything it did from matters of merely local importance to issues of global relevance.

Taiwan under Chiang Kai-shek

Chiang built his relationship with the US to endure, despite the many setbacks that it would undergo. His confidence in an ultimate reunification with China in the Nationalists' favour

47

survived the loss of Taiwan's seat at the United Nations in 1971 when a majority of other member states voted to replace it with the People's Republic. It endured the even greater disaster of America's rapprochement under Nixon with the Communists in Beijing in 1972 – a move principally motivated by the Chinese and Americans' mutual loathing of the Soviet Union.

There was nothing wholly inevitable about the outcome of each of these events for Taiwan. In the case of the first, Chiang did have the option of continuing Taiwanese representation at the UN, just as South and North Korea both had seats there. The main effect of the UN vote was Taiwan's loss of its prized permanent slot on the Security Council. Despite this, a new seat for Taiwan in the General Assembly was a possibility. But so offensive did Chiang regard the suggestion of sharing any space with the people he called the 'Communist bandits' that he labelled the UN a 'shameful organization' and a 'den of iniquity'. He ordered the Taiwanese delegation in New York to withdraw from UN membership.[12]

The same principle applied to the second issue, the conferring of diplomatic recognition on Taiwan by other nations. Those nations that decided to grant at least some recognition of Beijing were immediately ostracized by Chiang. Neither Beijing nor Taiwan allowed any country that formally recognized one of them as a sovereign independent nation to do the same for the other. This meant that despite the rapprochement between Beijing and Washington in 1972, the possibility of the US recognizing both sides of the strait was never an option. For a few years, the US maintained a balancing act by having formal diplomatic ties with Taipei and informal ones with Beijing. But by 1979 it was forced to reverse its position and formally recognize the People's Republic instead.

This impetuous attitude by Chiang and his government

towards Taiwan's increasingly isolated position ran parallel with a harsh approach to domestic governance of the island. Despite continuous expressions of dissent amongst some parts of the population and demands for a greater political voice, Chiang deployed an iron fist. The era of martial law, which was imposed in 1949, lasted for thirty-eight years. Although village-level elections were permitted, the Nationalist Party sat atop everything and controlled what mattered to it, from the legal system – where it appointed all judges – to the core strategic industries. Until his final years, Chiang presided over a system that was every bit as autocratic and intolerant of domestic opposition as the regime of his fellow dictator Mao Zedong, albeit less epically disastrous in terms of loss of human life.

That Chiang was able to safeguard the existence of Taiwan and steer it towards relative stability by the late 1950s was partly because he had advantages, despite losing the Civil War, that the mainland regime didn't. The first was the growing economic alliance with the US, which gave US$1.4 billion in aid to the island from 1951 to 1965.[13] This was used to lay the foundations of a modern economy. Ironically, Chiang, who had been regarded as an incompetent economist when presiding over the whole of China before 1949, became a far more efficient leader when put in charge of the smaller territory of the island. By the early 1970s, prosperity and living standards were improving dramatically. Taiwan was becoming one of the most successful economies in the region, with real gross domestic product (GDP – the total value of all goods and services within an economy) increasing by 10 per cent on average each year from 1950 to 1970.[14] Over this period, the island became a globally important exporter. Plentiful reserves of cheap, highly educated labour contributed to the nurturing of semi-high-tech and other manufacturing industries, which helped achieve such rapid development.

This supplied Chiang with his second great blessing. While Taiwan was repressive and often violent and troublesome to those who dared to overtly oppose its government, it was by no means as riddled by fear and subject to conflict as the Communist state to the north. As the world watched the chaos of the Cultural Revolution sweep across the mainland during the 1960s and 1970s, Taiwan was a far less worrying story to Western eyes. Its population was at least enjoying improved living conditions and greater material well-being as a result of the economic changes happening. While emphatically not a democracy, nor was it some vast despotic behemoth where teenage Red Guards led mass campaigns to humiliate and beat up schoolteachers, as was happening in the People's Republic. The contrast earned Taiwan a more benign, favourable image with the outside world, amongst both policymakers and the general public. It was seen as an ally, a friend – 'Free China', as its supporters in the US called it. The era of there being a 'good China' and a 'bad China' had started.

Taiwan's Years in the Wilderness: The 1970s

Subsequent events showed that it was just as well that Taiwan had developed its economy and its international reputation. The 1970s were increasingly tough years. After the worst period of repression in the 1950s and 1960s, and before the moves to reform and democratize that began in the 1980s, the island weathered a harsher environment as China became more active on the international stage, and other countries started to shift their diplomatic recognition to Beijing.

For many Taiwanese, these were years of betrayal, when the US – despite those on the island believing it had promised otherwise – withdrew much of its support. This largely coincided with the rise in America of an attitude towards international relations based on national self-interest rather than on a commitment to more abstract values and ideas such as freedom and support for the spread of democracy. Academic turned National Security Advisor Henry Kissinger was the intellectual architect of this, with his political master, President Richard Nixon, the overlord. For them, the 800 million people of the People's Republic could not be ignored and left outside the confines of the global system. They were also keen to secure Mao's China as a counterbalance to the place they both regarded as the greater threat: the Soviet Union. In this great game, Taiwan figured only as a secondary consideration.

Kissinger as good as washed America's hands of security and political responsibility for the long-term future of the island when he spoke with Chinese leaders during his visit to Beijing in 1972. The One China policy, in its American version, was constructed in this atmosphere. While not yet conferring full diplomatic recognition on the People's Republic, the Shanghai Communiqué of 1972, signed when Nixon was in the country on his historic trip, acknowledged Beijing's demand that there was only one China and that the PRC was it. 'Acknowledge' is not a strong statement of support, however. One can acknowledge that a friend thinks the world is flat, while also believing they are insane for doing so. But in the Chinese version, the language is slightly stronger – with 'chengren' implying greater support for what is being talked about than its usual English translation, 'acknowledges'. On this delicate use of language, diplomatic space was built for America to try to manage its commitments to its new partner, the PRC, while still seeming to stand by its older one in Taipei.

With America transferring its full diplomatic recognition

from Taiwan to China on the first day of 1979, Taiwan had never been so isolated since 1949. It was also receiving more criticism for its lack of political reform and its harsh management of domestic dissent. Around the same time that protests were occurring against autocratic political systems in South Korea and Eastern Europe, an incident in the southern port city of Kaohsiung in December 1979 saw activists arrested while demonstrating for greater democratic and human rights. Initially, the Taiwanese government adopted a hard line: long sentences were handed out to those involved. In early 1980, one member of the emerging opposition movement imprisoned after Kaohsiung, Lin Yi-hsiung, tragically saw two of his three daughters and his mother brutally killed under suspicious circumstances, even as his home was under close surveillance by the authorities. The case remains unsolved to this day, with heavy suspicion falling on the security services. But it was symptomatic of the societal tensions Taiwan faced during this period: many members of the public distrusted and were hostile to the state and its agents, which they saw as deploying outrageous levels of violence and coercion against them. The thriving economy might have changed people's lives, but the political system remained ossified and outdated.

China too was transforming. At the end of 1978, new leadership around the rehabilitated veteran politician Deng Xiaoping started to discreetly dismantle Maoist-style rule. Economic reforms were launched. Some of these duplicated elements of the Taiwanese model. The vast labour pool in China started to manufacture, in specially designated zones, for the outside world. This move in itself placed competitive pressure on Taiwan. There were even hopes of political reform on the mainland during the 1980s. In view of all these economic and social changes, while Taiwan could have persisted with a largely one-party system, the social and diplomatic costs of doing so were becoming increasingly steep.

The process that was to lead to the dramatic democratic changes of the 1990s was initiated in the previous decade by Chiang Kai-shek's successor as Taiwan's leader, and also his only legitimate son, Chiang Ching-kuo. This was unexpected – although the fact that, for part of his youth, the younger Chiang was a virulent critic and opponent of his father was perhaps a harbinger of his future capricious nature. In his early years, he lived for a time in the Soviet Union, where he married a Russian, Faina Ipatyevna Vakhreva. She was to assume the Chinese name Chiang Fang-liang and be the first lady of the Republic of China on Taiwan from 1978 to 1988.

On Chiang Ching-kuo's return to China in 1937, however, he operated as one of the elder Chiang's right-hand men and as an enforcer of his policies. Gordon Kerr, the American observer, described him as the chief enabler of the repression and terror implemented under Chiang Kai-shek's rule after 1949, with responsibility for the dreaded security services. It was Chiang Ching-kuo who sanctioned the attempts to silence the early agitators for democratic reform, such as the academic Peng Ming-min. Peng spent two years under house arrest until he fled the country in 1970; he then lived in exile in the US for a number of years, before standing in the 1996 presidential election against Lee Teng-hui.

Chiang Ching-kuo, however, underwent a Damascene conversion in the final months before his death in January 1988. He ordered the lifting of martial law after nearly four decades and finally permitted opposition political parties to openly register. The most significant of these, the Democratic Progressive Party, had already gained its first seats in the 1986 legislative elections by standing candidates as independents; now it began to campaign in local elections under its own banner.[15] Chiang also appointed a native Taiwanese, Lee Teng-hui, as his successor rather than one of the mainlanders who had previously dominated the Nationalist Party.

Taiwan proved fertile ground for democracy. Perhaps the centuries in which weary central authorities had castigated the island for its state of perpetual ferment and opposition to external rule helped it flourish, in that democracy finally provided a manageable outlet for these internal disagreements. Taiwanese had rebelled against the Dutch, the Qing, the Japanese and the Nationalist Party rulers from the mainland. From the 1980s, they started rebelling against themselves. But they did so using mostly peaceful means, through elections fought on the basis of universal adult suffrage. These took place first in 1991 and 1992 for the Legislative Assembly (Taiwan's lower house, established in 1947 with 760 members, but reduced at this time to 161), and then for the presidency in 1996. This ensured that by 2000, when the first peaceful transition of power from one political party to another took place, the island had taken a less traumatic and violent path than other countries to becoming a fully democratic nation.

History and Local Identity

History matters enormously in Taiwan today. It is not just an academic issue, about a past that is over and can be regarded with equanimity. Instead it lives on in the memories of people, informing their sense of who they are and where they have come from, as well as in their emotions. At times, the interpretation of past episodes such as the 228 Event has been so contentious that public discussion has turned violent. Attempts to create a stronger sense of local history and narratives during the 'Taiwanization' campaigns of the early 2000s were controversial and opposed by many.

A lot of this is due to the fact that Taiwan became a divided society as a result of the mass migration of mainland people when the Nationalists were defeated in the Civil War, creating deep fissures between those who had lived on Taiwan for generations and the newcomers. Each side had different stories to tell and a starkly different understanding of where they belonged and who they were. In the early years, these fissures were dealt with by force and repression. The 228 Event is a great symbol of this, an incident where locals and outsiders clashed, but which was then erased from public memory until the government apologized for it in 1995. The stored-up feelings of resentment and anger that followed this lengthy period of repression became apparent when liberalization finally happened, giving birth to a far sharper, stronger sense of local identity once it was finally allowed free expression. More and more people saw themselves as 'different' and interpreted the history they had experienced accordingly. Historians like Su Beng produced accounts that made clear that the story of the island was not some adjunct to the great narratives subscribed to on the mainland across the water. Taiwan was a place with its own unique tale to tell which needed to be understood on its own terms.

In Su Beng's account, there was the 400-year period when a specific form of local consciousness and identity was nurtured. This created the idea of a place where people had come not to take refuge under the shadow of their former home, but to develop something new and fresh. Like the founders of the United States, these early Taiwanese laid the cornerstones for an island which was a place of alternative Chineseness. There was also recognition of the deep layers of other histories – the indigenous people and their stories. These too reinforced the sense that Taiwan was different.

As the first chapter showed, that process of retelling created deeper differences from mainland China. In the early decades, the Nationalists maintained the hope that one day what had been sundered by the Civil War would be reunited again. Reunification was viable to them because it *was* underlain by the idea that there was something once unified that could be put back together. But by the 1970s, this dream had faded. Years of pursuing such different paths had created two societies and two outlooks which, if they ever had been deeply conjoined (a highly debatable point), were now far more separate. The question this posed the outside world, with increasing urgency and pressure, was what to do about it: recognize this separation and come closer to treating Taiwan as completely different? Or continue with the convenient fiction that nothing was changing and carry on as things were?

The Taiwan conundrum of today was created in this historical moment. Understanding how that happened helps in appreciating the nature of the problem that exists now. But it gives no clues to a solution, for the simple reason that many features of the current situation are unprecedented. The world has never seen a China as economically advanced and powerful as exists today. Nor has it ever seen a politically reformed, modernized Taiwan. There are faint signs, suggestions, hints scattered in the past, but no strong lines or trends indicating where things will go. The one thing the island's history does show is that unplanned, accidental events have had huge impacts. Taiwan's status today is emphatically not the result of foresight and design. The issue is whether one day in the future something unexpected and unforeseen will either resolve the status of the island or pitch it into grave crisis. In that respect, history offers little comfort, and much cause for caution. That is perhaps the sole lesson that can be learned from it.

3. Becoming Taiwanese: Democracy in Action

At about thirteen degrees centigrade, it's what passes for a cold evening in Taipei. But the crowd assembling before the imposing Presidential Office Building in the centre of the city soon warms up. A rock group is playing a loud medley of songs, mostly on the theme of hope and being proud to be Taiwanese. Sam Yang, the lead singer, roars out, 'Let me stand up like a Taiwanese', in English, before the lyrics drift back into the local Taiwanese dialect. When he's done, and the audience applaud, waving the small green flags they've been given, and are sitting down on small red stools again, two speakers are announced. They are candidates for the legislative elections to be held in two days' time, on 13 January, who troop on to the stage and start their pitch by launching an attack on their opponents. Those people on the other side of the political spectrum 'love China, not Taiwan', they shout into their microphones. 'All they're interested in is gullibly swallowing the empty promises of the larger, northern neighbour.' They've forgotten, one of them shouts, about how 'freedom is never given freely but *earned*'. Taiwan is a democracy, in charge of its own fate, its own destiny, its own space; this is something it has fought hard for and should never forget.

Today is the final stretch of the 2024 election campaign. Presidential elections are held every four years on the island, at the same time as those for the Legislative Assembly. This rally is for the ruling DPP presidential candidate and is being held in one of the sacred spaces in the fight for multiparty politics, universal adult suffrage and free elections – a place now called Liberty Square. Later on, a speaker explains the meaning of where we are all sitting: it is where demonstrators came during the years when the other main party, the Nationalists, allowed no rivals and locked up those who opposed them. How could anyone vote for those people nowadays, when they have an actual choice, one of the final speakers shouts, while photos recalling the years of the White Terror and the decades of martial law are displayed on the huge LED screens on either side of the stage.

Over the previous two months, progress to this final rally of the 2024 election, which 200,000 people attended, was turbulent and rocky. The DPP, in power since 2016, was enjoying a fortunate split in its opposition. On the one hand stood the party's old nemesis, the Nationalists. On the other, a new force had appeared, led by a former member of the DPP, Ko Wen-je. Frustrated at some of the party's policies while mayor of the capital, he set up his own organization, the Taiwan People's Party (TPP). A popular, charismatic figure, he'd gathered support particularly from the young, who were tired of what they saw as the same old, stale two-party confrontational politics. That he'd worked for years as a doctor meant he was trusted and looked up to. Initial polling put him almost equal with the other, far better-established candidates. He looked like threatening a major upset.

At the DPP's final rally, though, the reason why it directed its rhetorical fire at the Nationalists rather than Ko's new party was due to events that had occurred at the end of the previous year. A strange episode in November saw an attempt by Ko and the Nationalists, led by their presidential candidate Hou Yu-yi, to create a coalition. Both were united in wanting better relations with the mainland and believed that this provided a basis for linking up together. Had they pulled it off, there was a good chance they would have attracted enough disaffected voters to get a simple majority. In a first-past-the-post election, that was all that was needed to win the presidency. The negotiations went on for a few weeks, but on 18 November, they sputtered out for good over arguments about who would lead the coalition and who would be standing as the vice-presidential running mate. Both sides produced polls from telephone canvassing they had undertaken to prove they had the greater support, but neither side agreed with the other's methodology. At a chaotic final press conference, both withdrew from the proposed deal. From this moment, the Nationalists reverted to being the main opposition party again, and therefore the chief target of DPP ire.

Watching the rally unfold on 11 January, it is easy to feel the drama and excitement of democracy, Taiwanese style. The atmosphere is almost festive. A series of promotional videos burnish the credentials of the DPP's candidate, William Lai Ching-te. His running mate, Hsiao Bi-khim, is greeted with roars when she strides on to the stage, late into the evening. Some people in the audience hold up placards with cartoon cats on them, a reference to her persona as a 'cat warrior' standing up to the so-called 'wolf warriors' in Beijing – the term used since 2021 for the aggressively vocal supporters of nationalism, both online and in public, in the People's Republic. Following one of the themes of the evening, she launches into an attack on the former president, Ma Ying-jeou, a man who, she says in mock disbelief, told his compatriots after a recent visit to China that they should 'trust Xi Jinping'. A picture of him and the Chinese leader flashes up on the huge screens. There are screams of indignation. 'Trust Team Taiwan,' she belts out, setting off a chant that echoes across the huge crowd.

As these calls fade away, the final two speakers with star billing make their appearance. Tsai Ing-wen, president for the previous eight years, now reaching the end of her permitted term in power, comes out to massive fanfare. Her pitch is straightforward. 'Sure, we have done some things that people were not happy with,' she says calmly, standing at a podium. 'Yes, there were always things we could have done better, or quicker. Things can always be improved.' Then, leaning a little towards the microphone and speaking to the hushed crowd, her voice rises. 'But every single day of the last eight years, I can tell you one thing. We have always, *always* been moving forward. Every single day, we have made progress. Let us carry on; let us carry Taiwan forward. Vote for William Lai, and he will do this for you, every minute of every day.' And with that, the man she speaks of, who has been her deputy since 2020, William Lai Ching-te, appears by her side. Holding up his hand, she presents him to the crowd as someone she trusts, supports and wants to see elected.

The Long and Winding Road to Taiwanese Democracy

Taiwan, for its many supporters in the West, exemplifies the fairy tale of the End of History – the theory made famous by the American political scientist Francis Fukuyama that the end of the Cold War heralded the permanent victory of liberal democracy over totalitarianism. This is a place where, after a heroic struggle lasting decades, the people's will for free votes and full democracy prevailed, and events like the 2024 rally I attended became possible. Many, however, were sceptical in the early years after elections started happening that they would prove sustainable and long-lasting. They pointed to the fact that waves of democratization were all too often followed elsewhere by the dominance of one party and the gradual erosion of democratic processes (Russia is one example; Turkey and Hungary might prove to be others). But today, the theorists and promoters of democracy as the ultimate, best form of governance can look to the island as a textbook success story.

Taiwan's democracy since the end of the twentieth century has certainly become a critical part of the identity of the island. It has always been diverse and vibrant. In 1990, during the era when democratic processes for the legislative elections were being set up, there was the infamous case of stripper and adult entertainer Hsu Shao-tan, who tried to stand on a platform of extreme liberalism. She ended up being defeated. But the fact that she was able to participate was a sign of things to come. Today, myriad smaller parties promote niche causes, many of their candidates with lifestyles and programmes as colourful and different as Hsu was. Green politics has also come to the island. There are an estimated 160 other political parties, all competing in a plethora of different local and national elections. Democracy showcases the variety and vitality of Taiwanese society. It is increasingly its greatest soft-power asset. A non-democratic Taiwan would be ignored. A democratic one cannot be sacrificed. That is why this island is the quandary it is in the twenty-first century. Values and ideals mean it is an indispensable ally. Its defeat by China would not just be a territorial and economic catastrophe, but would be seen by some as an ideological and even moral one.

The 2024 election proved to be one of the most dramatic since the first was held back in 1996. Part of this was because the candidates were competing for office in a situation with a unique combination of local and external issues. On the one hand, they needed to have proposals about how to manage the economy and improve living standards in the face of the challenges posed by rising inflation and cost of living, which would be familiar to voters everywhere else and which had grown dramatically more worrying for the electorate as growth slowed from 2022. But, on the other hand, there was the great external issue looming over everything else: cross-strait relations. Taiwanese voters have to cast their ballot aware that the consequences might not just be changes in local policies, but could trigger major ruptures in geopolitics. They are voters in national elections with global significance.

As elsewhere in the world in recent years, the divisions amongst voters over issues from economic management and the role of the state to social mores and values have grown deeper and the space for compromise between different sides of the debate far narrower. The three main parties contending in 2024 offered a conventional choice. The DPP was promising to maintain its strong commitment to Taiwan's autonomy. Its candidate, William Lai Ching-te, is probably the most enthusiastic supporter of this strand of politics, declaring earlier in his career that Taiwan was de facto independent, even though he then had to qualify his statement to appease at least some in the country and the outside world worried about the consequences of his words. The Nationalists and TPP were advocating the need for security through dialogue and engagement with the mainland. The opinion polls throughout the final months of the campaign showed that none of the three main parties was winning the support of much more than a third of the electorate. As in many other places since the mid-2000s – from the US to countries in Europe – Taiwan was displaying a system trying to accommodate the very different demands of the people it governed, and often struggling.

It's not just in the drama of huge rallies that one can see the deep importance of democracy on the island. It's also there on the most intimate level. I was having lunch with a family only a week before the day of the vote, when one person at the table joked that there were supporters of *all* the main parties present. The younger diners liked Ko Wen-je and his brand of 'new politics' trying to break the old two-party dominance and force through a new player, the TPP. The older ones, who remembered the long struggle for democracy, supported the DPP and the Nationalists in almost equal measure. For the middle-aged, the issue of mainland relations weighed heavily, not least because of China's continuing economic importance. Either way, it was remarkable to see how deeply people had embraced competitive politics – how they traded stories about particular political figures and were so passionate about the simple act of going to cast a vote for them, as if these individuals were personal family friends.

To arrive at this point, where a family could openly and amicably discuss their different political preferences together, Taiwan has travelled a long, hard path. It was also a unique one. The seeds of participatory politics were present from very early on. There were local elections held with multiple candidates, something that started at the very end of the era of Japanese rule in an attempt to recruit at least some of the local population to soft support for the alien regime. But the end of Japanese rule after defeat in the Second World War marked the disappearance, within a few years, of these very modest steps towards some form of public participation in decision-making.

The beginning of rule under the Nationalists meant a new form of governance, where there was the mirage of electoral politics but without any underlying reality. Polls were held at village and provincial level. These were highly manipulated by the ruling party and the central government. Local elites were allowed to dominate, sometimes with support from the secret societies which involved the mafia, sometimes from clan or family networks. They presented themselves as not aligned to the Nationalists, and neutral in their political leanings; but in the end, they wholly supported the ruling party's aims and its dominance in society. Any other elections – those at island-wide (and therefore national) level – had only Nationalist candidates. No officials with powers over budgets or administrative affairs were selected by ballot.

One of the great oddities of the Taiwanese experience is that the one partially democratic election it held, where a Legislative Yuan (or Assembly) of over 700 members was appointed, did not take place solely on the island, but across the whole of the rest of China. The 1948 national vote had every province represented. But the Assembly had barely convened before the Civil War swept the country away. The whole body fled with the Nationalist forces to Taiwan in 1949. There, for the next four decades until wholesale reform, it solemnly perpetuated the fiction that it was the legitimate, popularly appointed parliament with a nationwide remit. That the nation no longer existed in the form that it had when the members were elected was conveniently ignored. For decades, officials in Taiwan ostensibly with responsibilities for massive mainland provinces like Henan, Guangdong and Sichuan carried on their illusory business, often thousands of kilometres from the places they were supposed to be representing. Having no authority over the rest of China, the Republic on Taiwan could not hold meaningful follow-up elections. By the 1970s, there were some reforms when the Legislative Assembly assumed most of the powers previously enjoyed by the National Assembly; established in 1947, this entity operated like the US Senate, and also appointed the president and vice president. Before this shake-up, the membership of both bodies operated largely like a shadow government of a non-existent realm. What's more, many representatives had started slowly dying off. Occasionally, new appointments were made in an ad hoc fashion. But the pool of people with any direct memory of mainland affairs shrank, raising even more questions about the purpose of this entity.

The real national government was the Taiwanese provincial one – a further example of how, in the case of Taiwan, what the label says rarely indicates exactly what is in the bottle. The provincial governor of Taiwan (sometimes also called the Chairman of the Provincial Government) was, to all intents and purposes, the main administrator of the territory that the government in Taipei actually controlled; while their ostensibly higher counterpart, the premier of the Republic of China, spent most of their time pretending they were running a territory they no longer had any authority over. The constitution too was ostensibly that of the whole country of China, not just the province of Taiwan, even though it only had validity and any kind of reality in the latter, which was by now operating increasingly like a fully fledged sovereign state. To add a final layer of confusion, the People's Republic of China regarded any attempts to remove references to the 'Republic of China' and replace them simply with 'Taiwan' as heresy, and akin to an act of war. Behind Beijing's great bugbear was its aim not only to see the Republic of China completely disappear but, before it vanished, to acknowledge it had no legitimacy (even over the territory of Taiwan it was holding out on) and to cede everything back to the rightful successor government in the north. As a result, the Taiwanese ended up with a model of governance, and a name for their homeland (Republic of

China), that bore no relationship to the real world – which naturally complicated and confused things.

The development of democracy on Taiwan since the 1970s has been the story not just of countless activists and individuals who supported the move to a multiparty, representative system, but also of five key figures. Chiang Ching-kuo is the first, even though Taiwan did not function as a democracy under his leadership. But he deserves recognition as the instigator who provided the platform for future change by tolerating other political parties rather than just the Nationalists, even if they were not granted full formal recognition. This allowed for the flourishing of democracy, and for its development by those coming after him. Lee Teng-hui was the first native Taiwanese to become president, and the first to be democratically elected to that position, in 1996. Chen Shui-bian, his successor, was the first to lead the opposition party, the DPP, to victory in a presidential election and achieve the transfer of power from the Nationalists, in 2000. Later, Ma Ying-jeou for the Nationalists and Tsai Ing-wen of the DPP have largely been consolidators. But they have ruled in the crucial period when many democracies have shown signs of fraying and fragmentation. Their contribution in strengthening the processes and institutions of democracy, respecting electoral outcomes, and allowing the peaceful transfer of power between opposing parties has been critical.

Beyond individuals, there were also two key factors that laid the initial foundations of modern democracy. The first was social change. Hopes of reunification with the mainland under a Nationalist victory had long receded, and divisions in society between mainlanders and local Taiwanese (as noted in the previous chapters) grew less sharp. Society was far harder to control and to dictate to because of people's improved financial circumstances. Economic development created a tax-paying middle class, well educated, well travelled, and full of expectations and opinions. Unions in particular played a key role, pushing back against government restrictions and demanding stronger working rights and better terms and conditions. Civil society burgeoned. The formation of illegal, but quietly tolerated, political parties in the mid-1980s, and the large uptake in their public support and membership, meant it was almost only a matter of time before they had to be granted space in society, rather than being ignored or repressed.

The second key factor was America's shift of diplomatic recognition to China in 1979. Taiwan's new isolation meant it had to take remedial action. One such measure was to accelerate and bolster its economic performance so that the country grew wealthier and more interconnected through trade and business with the outside world. In this way, it could create a strong international presence, despite lacking (in the eyes of most) the status of a nation, and so reinforce its relations with the rest of the world in order to counterbalance the influence of China. While not the principal driver of the democracy movement, becoming a liberal, multiparty, popularly elected system created a powerful new political bond with the US when other formal ties between the two, such as diplomatic treaties and security guarantees, were lacking.

Lee Teng-hui: The Man for All Seasons

Lee Teng-hui has good grounds for being named the real father of Taiwanese democracy. He was an unexpected choice as Chiang Ching-kuo's successor in 1988. A native Taiwanese, someone who had been brought up in the colonial era when

Japanese was the main language, he did not remotely fit the stereotype of an elite leader of the Nationalist Party, which was previously dominated by mainlanders. Indeed, opponents attacked him both as too pro-Japanese and pro-local Taiwanese when he came to power.

Lee's background was certainly a rich and complex one. Educated initially in Japan, he served in the Imperial Japanese Army towards the end of the Second World War in Asia, as did many of his generation. Around this time, he joined the Communist Party of China, but only briefly. He became an agricultural economist on his return to his native island, and was one of the first Taiwanese to study in the United States in the 1950s and 1960s, gaining a doctorate at Cornell University. It was as a specialist in agricultural reform that he started his political career, working as an official on plans to rationalize and modernize Taiwan's then crucially important farming sector.

Lee was a man of many identities. His world view was informed by his awareness of being Taiwanese, with a strong sense of Chinese culture; an equally powerful understanding of Japanese culture; a commitment to Christianity, after his conversion to Presbyterianism as an adult; a global outlook from his time in the US; and the ability to operate both as an academic and as a politician. Those many different guises meant that, despite his scholarly demeanour, he proved a wily and formidable opponent once empowered. It was also the reason why the Chinese, after assessing him as someone who might be trusted and engaged with, came to see him as tricky, evasive and dishonest. He was eventually to be expelled from his own party in 2001, around the time that some of his supporters were creating a new political movement, the Taiwan Solidarity Union.

Lee's various autobiographical writings show that he regarded his principal duty as safeguarding Taiwan's uniqueness and autonomy. 'Taiwan has a future,' he once stated, 'only if it exists.'[1] Any leader of the island, he wrote, must be 'someone who loves Taiwan deeply and will shed blood, sweat, and tears' for the place.[2] This passionate commitment prompted him to veer sometimes towards strong declarations, stating famously at one point that the relationship across the strait involved two states, not one.[3] His original opponents were the hardliners in the Nationalist Party itself, figures who regarded him with unease because of his background as a local. They may have originally felt they could easily manipulate him to continue to do their bidding. In this they were proved almost completely wrong.

Lee had discerned the significant changes happening in his own society – the ways in which economically, socially and culturally it was undergoing a fundamental metamorphosis. These were the things that shaped his political ideas going forward. The mainlanders were dwindling by the early 1990s to less than 10 per cent of the population. Their dominance in administration, governance and other areas of public life, something that had been eroding for years, was no longer defensible. In the case of the National Assembly mentioned above, he visited each and every one of the more than 600 members and got them to agree to vote for a change in the constitution which effectively removed them from any meaningful role in Taiwan's governance. The first fully democratic elections for the remaining Legislative Assembly were held in 1991, resulting in a significant number of DPP seats. While the presidential election of 1996 is often spoken of as the formal start of the island's democratic history, this earlier event was every bit as significant. For the first time, the island's legislature had democratic legitimacy: its members, standing for rival political parties and representing various groups, were elected by secret ballot on a one person, one vote universal franchise basis.

Some of Lee's moves were highly contentious. His appointment in the mid-1990s of Cassidy and Associates, a lobbying company in Washington, proved effective in securing strong support within the US Congress enabling a visit to America in 1995, when he addressed his old university. But the fact this occurred over the head of President Bill Clinton, who had originally vetoed Lee's tour, caused bad blood with the White House. As the politician Su Chi, who was a young advisor to Lee at the time, put it in his book about the era, this was a case of the tail (Taiwan) wagging two dogs (China and the US).[4] Taiwan was playing the US, assuming it would have to stand by the island's side if the Chinese grew too bellicose. That assumption proved correct when Chinese anger at the visit and at some of Lee's other actions immediately prompted military exercises in the strait, which triggered an American naval response. But, for the US government, the feeling of being manipulated was not a welcome one.

After Lee won an overwhelming majority in the first presidential election with full universal adult suffrage in 1996, he proved increasingly mercurial in office. In particular, his controversial description of Taiwan and China having state-to-state relations, mentioned earlier, was seen as a clear bid for recognition of the island's independence, and sent tensions between Taipei and Beijing rocketing once more. And while Lee did not stand for the presidency again in 2000, but stepped aside for younger Nationalist leaders such as his successor as chairman of the party, Lien Chan, he then promptly became involved with a new group, the Taiwan Solidarity Union, which advocated for independence. He maintained a lively and often contrarian commentary on domestic politics right up to his death in 2020, aged ninety-eight.

Lee was a divisive, complex figure, a man who aroused strong antipathy amongst the more conservative members of his own party who found that the policies and changes he implemented once he came to power ended up watering down the Nationalists' hold on power rather than defending it. For those in the outside world too, particularly in the US, he was regarded as a loose cannon, someone who was willing to try to exploit divisions in Washington in ways that seemed to play the US off against China. But Lee's achievement in moving Taiwan from a semi-democracy in the 1980s, where other political parties were tolerated but lacked formal legal protection, to full multiparty legislative and presidential elections a few years later, means his mark on history is significant. For someone born when his homeland was still a colony of Japan, that was a remarkable journey.

Chen Shui-bian: The Chancer and Transformer

Lee's successor as president, Chen Shui-bian, was from a wholly different background. While also native Taiwanese, his family was less well off than Lee's, and hailed from the countryside. Chen was educated on the island, rather than abroad, and he secured a place at the elite Taiwan University in Taipei. In the late 1970s, he was a rising star in the legal world, a brilliant lawyer who defended some of the activists prosecuted after the pro-human rights Kaohsiung Incident in 1979. Chen's wife was tragically paralysed for life in 1985 when she was run over several times by a farm vehicle. The Nationalist-controlled security services were suspected of instigating the attack, although this has never been proved. Chen himself became more active in DPP politics after the party was formally established in 1987, and he successfully stood to become mayor of Taipei in 1994. Four years later, he was defeated by his Nationalist opponent, Ma Ying-jeou. He used the following two years to prepare for his presidential bid in 2000.

Chen in his public career combined luck with guile. The 2000 election typified this. The Nationalist vote was split between the formal candidate, the somewhat stiff and uncharismatic Lien Chan, and the more unpredictable James Soong, who had left the governing party in the 1990s over anger at its failure to choose him as the successor to Lee Teng-hui. This single move ended up handing victory to the DPP. In a first-past-the-post electoral system, Chen's 39 per cent of the votes was enough to defeat his rivals Soong, who got 36 per cent, and Lien, who underwhelmed on 23 per cent. This ushered in the first peaceful transfer from the party in power to the opposition.

Although Chen became a hate figure in Beijing, where he was seen as a hardline agitator for independence, his position on Taiwanese sovereignty proved as supple and unpredictable as Lee's, though in different ways. His party contained people who believed passionately in Taiwan as a wholly separate country, but Chen himself was a realist, and knew that unilateral declarations would provoke China and alienate the US. His inaugural speech was a classic piece of lawyerly evasion, saying that *unless* his country was attacked, it would not declare independence and renounce its claims over the mainland, nor would it seek to rewrite the constitution and replace its mentions of the 'Republic of China' with 'Taiwan'. His actions, however, were regarded by some in the outside world as far more divisive. Unlike Lee, Chen had to work with a legislature and judiciary dominated by the opposition. He tried to address this by appointing both DPP and Nationalist ministers to his first cabinet. While a worthy gesture, ultimately it proved unworkable due to the two parties' political differences being too fundamental to manage.

Chen's re-election in 2004 was dramatic, with an attempted shooting in the final days of the campaign, before a razor-thin victory. This time, the opposition was unified, with Soong no longer standing and only Lien Chan fighting again for the Nationalists. Most polls showed Chen and his running mate, Annette Lu, were due to lose. While campaigning in Tainan only a few days before the actual vote, Chen was shot. The bullet wounded him in the stomach, but not seriously, with a second bullet grazing a plaster cast on Lu's leg. After a brief visit to a hospital for treatment, he was able to continue campaigning the same day. No one saw who actually fired the shots, but the controversy over who might have done so – and why – dominated the news agenda.

Conspiracy theories soon started to fly around. One claimed that Chen and his supporters had deliberately staged the event in order to give him a pretext to declare a state of emergency. That meant army and security officials, regarded as firm supporters of the Nationalists, would have had to work and would therefore be unable to vote. Others believed it was a means of garnering sympathy from the electorate. Chen himself portrayed the incident as an attack on the DPP and its chances of winning. To this day, the culprit who pulled the trigger has never been found, and no one was ever charged.

Chen sneaked through to victory by a margin of less than 0.02 per cent of the national vote. Despite this slenderest of majorities, once things settled down, his new administration was broadly accepted. The price for Chen personally, however, was hatred by his opponents that verged on the obsessive. His policy on cross-strait relations, with its insistence on Taiwan as an autonomous actor, was also regarded with increasing trepidation by both Beijing and Washington because of the instability it threatened. When Chen finally stood down as president in 2008, after the maximum two terms, his image was tarnished by claims of corruption, which also involved family members.

The Chen era was notable not so much for its domestic and foreign policy stances, but for the cultural change it witnessed. Chen's government supported what came to be labelled 'de-sinification': the replacement of language and symbols from the Chiang era, with their heavy associations with the mainland and their set idea of Chinese culture, with local ones that related far more to Taiwan and its own culture and history. A greater sense of Taiwanese identity was pursued in the educational curriculum: the history of Taiwan, rather than the Chinese dynasties, was promoted. Images and symbols associated with Chiang Kai-shek were removed, with the international airport which bore his name in Taoyuan, close to Taipei, being rebranded. These efforts were denounced by Beijing as attempts to foster separatism and undermine the common links between the two sides.

Chen's career after politics has been tragic. Almost as soon as the Nationalists assumed power they targeted him. The subject of a number of legal investigations, he was sentenced to life imprisonment in 2009 for bribery, money laundering and embezzlement, though this was reduced to twenty years in 2010. After an attempt at suicide three years later, and then serious health issues, he was granted parole on medical grounds in 2015. As part of the terms for his release, he was forbidden from commenting on political matters. Despite this, his significance for Taiwan's road to democracy is self-evident. He will be remembered as a major figure, one who showed that the political culture of the country was robust and inclusive enough to ensure power could be transferred peacefully.

Ma Ying-jeou: The Appeaser

Chen's successor as president, Ma Ying-jeou, was not a native Taiwanese. This became one of the vulnerabilities that his critics exploited when he stood in the presidential election of 2008. Born in Hong Kong, he was brought to Taiwan by his parents in the 1940s, when he was an infant. A student at the elite Taiwan University like his predecessor Chen, he subsequently went to Harvard and undertook a doctorate in law before returning to the island and serving as Minister of Justice in the 1990s under Lee Teng-hui. His enforcement of an anti-corruption campaign gave him the reputation of a clean politician who behaved with probity. This was something that stood him in good stead when he defeated the incumbent, Chen, in the 1998 Taipei mayoral race. Public anger at rising levels of corruption by political figures proved one of the election's main talking points. It made his background combatting such misconduct a strong basis for support.

Ma rebranded the Nationalist Party once he became its chairman in 2005, and achieved a surprise landslide comeback for his party during the presidential election in 2008. He accomplished this through a combination of charisma and a reputation for efficiency. This mattered, for the party he led was amongst the world's wealthiest political organizations, with over US$1 billion in assets, including buildings and land. The Nationalists had run Taiwan without challenge for so long that the boundary between what was theirs and what belonged to the state was entirely permeable. But Ma was one of the few figures of his generation who could appear as though he were above all this, because of his record supporting clean governance. He was also the only one who had enough credibility at the time – at least domestically – to craft a policy towards the mainland which was constructive and non-combative but also addressed Taiwanese security concerns.

Ma's eight years in power will probably be remembered as the high point of an attempt at more conciliatory and open-armed cross-strait relations. The approach was driven by the explosive growth of the PRC economy. Taiwanese, with economic problems mounting at home, needed to work out a way of joining in the Chinese growth feast without being eaten alive. Ma took risks, and went to the limits of his democratic mandate with the Economic Cooperation Framework Agreement of 2010. A partial free-trade agreement, it loosened up the flow of goods, and prepared the way for the future flow of services between the two sides of the strait. It meant that Taiwanese were able to enjoy beneficial commercial opportunities with the mainland, using it as a cheaper manufacturing and processing base. They were also able to place themselves at the heart of the China boom by utilizing their advantage of a shared language and at least some shared cultural values with the mainland in order to present Taiwanese companies as reliable partners for foreign enterprises that wanted to make things in China but did not know how to operate there. Soon Taiwanese businesses were constructing ever more massive factories in southern China, such as Foxconn, whose giant facilities pumped out iPhones for much of the world (and for the Chinese themselves), or the Taiwan Semiconductor Manufacturing Company, whose components power most of the globe's computers.

For someone who presented as sober and disciplined, Ma

proved a gambler. While his predecessors had leaned towards provocation and pushback against China, his strategy was to grow uncomfortably close with Taiwan's gigantic neighbour. He stood by the Nationalist philosophy of reunification as the eventual goal, but only when China had undergone political changes that aligned it with Taipei. This new iteration of the 'tail wagging the dog' was not lost on Beijing, but its response, under the low-key President Hu Jintao, was to forge ahead with an approach which, in its own words, combined the 'hard' and the 'soft'.[5] While continuing to wield a 'hard' stick, with the build-up along the southern coast of a formidable arsenal of ballistic missiles aimed across the strait, China also doled out plenty of 'soft' carrots, in the form of new investment and money-making opportunities offered to Taiwanese 'compatriots' – as Beijing called them – on a preferential basis.

As never before, Taiwan and China became open to each other. With direct flights permitted across the strait from 2010, every citizen who took the short journey served as a quasi-ambassador, representing the merits and attractions of their respective homes. Mainlanders in tour groups to Taiwan were exposed to the reality of life on the island, disseminating when they got back home a more positive image of a place they were used to being told was occupied by the enemy. And Taiwanese making the reverse journey were exposed to gleaming new cities, and to the results of three decades of breakneck modernization and development, as exemplified by Shanghai. Taiwan and China advertised themselves to each other in a mutual charm offensive, putting on their best behaviour and wearing their broadest smiles.

This campaign to change local hearts and minds on the island ended largely due to the mounting uneasiness and reservations of young Taiwanese. With no direct memories of the mainland, and weaker feelings towards it, they were more concerned by lack of decent employment opportunities, and soaring property prices at home – some of which was put down to the distorting influence of mainland investment driving up prices. This was supplemented by worries about Chinese enterprises buying up Taiwanese media companies, and then flooding cyberspace with propaganda, fake news and inducements in order to manipulate viewers, a problem that became the focus of passionate public discussion. Restrictions were soon put in place to try to vet this sort of ownership and prevent such influencing happening. As in other parts of the world, the perception that China was trying to control people's ideas – irrespective of whether it was indeed seeking to do so – culminated in heightened distrust and antagonism, rather than brainwashing.

This was one of the main reasons why demonstrations spread across the island in 2014 when Ma tried to move forward with a common investment agreement with China which would allow greater cooperation in the wide-ranging services sector (constituting more than two thirds of Taiwan's GDP). These protests came to be labelled the 'Sunflower Movement'. In April that year, some of the protestors managed to storm the Legislative Assembly, forcing members to pause their business. They occupied it for almost a fortnight before being expelled (and some promptly prosecuted). This expression of anger and frustration stopped the passage of the investment agreement into law.

While Ma continued with his policy of engagement and rapprochement with the mainland, going on to hold a historic meeting with Xi Jinping in 2015, the message from Taiwan's population was clear. Once Ma retired, they voted his former opponent Tsai Ing-wen into the presidency with a huge majority. Ma's vision of a world where the Taiwanese and Chinese could agree to disagree and push their differences over the horizon while they pragmatically engaged with one another economically was already losing its potency. As we will see in Chapter 5, Xi Jinping was a different leader to Hu – more assertive and charismatic, and promoting a far stronger brand of Chinese nationalism. The wider world was changing too: the West was bothered and bewildered by its financial woes since the 2008 economic crisis, and by its security challenges in the Middle East since the War on Terror following the 9/11 terrorist attacks, and the long, unsuccessful conflicts in Afghanistan and Iraq. Ma himself might regard his time in office as a missed opportunity, the last chance to create the softest of soft frameworks for cross-strait relations, where there was unity but also space for division. There is a strong chance he may well figure as the last Nationalist leader of the island. In 2024, his successors lost their third election in a row. Ma, however, persisted with his conviction that speaking to China was the right thing, meeting Xi again in April 2024, though this time he had long been out of power.

Tsai Ing-wen: She Stoops to Conquer

Tsai Ing-wen's appearance might tempt political opponents to underestimate her. A bespectacled cat-lover with a soft voice and a calm manner, she resembled nothing so much as the academic she once was. But with her election as president in 2016, this DPP politician proved herself a formidable operator: tough-minded, tactful, extremely pragmatic, yet someone who caught and channelled the public mood. At a time of loud-mouthed public figures with glib answers to intractable problems, Tsai was far from typical. The world should be relieved that she was in office at such a challenging time. Anyone more easily flummoxed or hot-tempered could have made bad missteps. In the end, on the big calls, Tsai's judgement proved sure.

A native of Taiwan, Tsai completed a doctorate at the London School of Economics before returning home to pursue her career. She served first as a trade negotiator, when the country was applying to join the World Trade Organization; and then, during Chen Shui-bian's first presidency, between 2000 and 2004, as head of the Mainland Affairs Council – the body established to promote exchange with China – where she was seen as a strong supporter of independence. Her past record while serving on the council and the stance she took in refusing to engage with the '1992 Consensus' (where both sides of the strait recognized there was only one China, but differed on how they defined it) were credited with contributing to her failure against Ma in 2012, the first time she ran for president. Maybe that lesson made her aware of the dangers of becoming too embroiled in policy on China. While she refused to pursue the path of Ma and pretend that economic alignment with the mainland had no downside, neither did she believe in adventurism and provocation. Returning to policies of the Lee era, she adopted a more proactive diplomacy, rebranding it as the New Southbound Policy. While the label for the policy was novel, it revisited aims first set out two decades before, when links were forged with other countries in the region rather than China in a bid to diversify the island's trade and investment options.

Facing the overwhelmingly male-dominated political elite in Beijing, Tsai was able to garner a great deal of unexpected extra support from the international community because China's behaviour seemed shrill and intimidating against someone so polite and restrained. Nowhere was this more obvious than over the unfolding situation in Hong Kong, which was a central theme of Tsai's years in power. Hong Kong's status as a special administrative region was originally intended as a model of the 'One Country, Two Systems' rubric crafted for Taiwan in the early 1980s, but by the 2010s its position had eroded to such an extent that the local leadership were largely seen as Beijing's puppets. The perception of weakening autonomy was confirmed when attempts to bring about promised reforms for the election of the chief executive – the most senior official in the city – collapsed in 2014. Beijing abruptly ended the fierce debate by saying Hong Kong had to accept the system the Chinese central government proposed. That involved a specially appointed electoral council approving whoever was put forward as a potential candidate, with the powers to veto anyone they didn't like. The flaws in this democratic model were self-evident, with representatives from more independent-minded parties having little to no chance of making it through to the final ballot.

Taiwanese watched as protestors occupied the centre of Hong Kong at the height of the dispute. They were right to be impressed by the spectacle. I passed through Hong Kong late that year and remember gazing down from the calm refuge of a skyscraper's upper floor at the lights, tents and protestors massed below. Unlike Taiwan's Sunflower Movement, Hong Kong's Umbrella Protests – so-called because of the way participants protected themselves with brollies from the heavy rain and from surveillance by the security services as they marched – were not so peacefully resolved. Increasingly large and violent confrontations continued sporadically until 2019, with a new security law passed to align the city with Beijing's demands for greater and more public displays of loyalty to the mainland the following year. These protests were met with correspondingly brutal displays of local government power, fully backed up by the Chinese central government. In the end, an electoral committee of 1,500 members directly appointed by Beijing was set up in 2021 despite the local opposition. John Lee, a new leader with a security background, was installed in 2022, having secured 99 per cent of the vote of this new body; he was the only candidate allowed to run, a sign of Beijing's clear support. Hong Kongese left the city in growing numbers as they witnessed the tightening of Xi's diktat, with over 160,000 moving to the UK alone between 2021 and 2024.

For Taiwanese, a key moment was the tragic episode in which a Hong Kongese tourist, Chan Tong-kai, was accused of murdering his pregnant girlfriend, Amber Poon Hiu-wing, also from Hong Kong, when on a holiday in Taipei in 2018. He fled home after depositing her body in a suitcase in bushes close to the hotel where they had been staying. When the body was found, the Taiwanese authorities requested that Chan be returned to face questioning. The response of their Hong Kong counterparts was to propose legislation that would allow extradition for the first time, and would cover not just Hong Kong and Taiwan but the whole of China. It opened up the possibility of Hong Kongese and Taiwanese for the first time being subject to mainland justice, and in theory being transported from their own legal jurisdictions into that of China to face charges. Those who had experienced the Chinese legal system, either as business people or through the criminal justice pathway, knew how harsh it was and hard to deal with. For Hong Kongese, who had assumed that their legal rights had been guaranteed as part of the retrocession agreement with Britain in 1997, the proposed removal of their immunity from the mainland's jurisdiction was a huge retrograde step. During the ensuing wrangle between Hong Kong, Taiwan and the People's Republic, the alleged murderer was able to avoid returning to Taiwan for police interview. To this day, he remains at large in Hong Kong. After huge public opposition, the extradition law itself was dropped by the Hong Kong government in October 2019.

While all this was going on, the main concern of Taiwanese was their stagnant economy. Dissatisfaction with the government's efforts to remedy this was reflected in low polling numbers for Tsai. She was accused of not doing enough to support growth, with division and discontent in her own party between those who wanted a more hardline stance on China, and those who desired more flexibility and trade with it. The same dissatisfaction with globalization that had shaken European and American politics also played a role. There was anger at rising inequality in society, at local industry's exposure to competition that destroyed jobs, and at the struggle of younger people to buy a house and establish their lives.

However, her response to the events in Hong Kong was one area where Tsai garnered plaudits from the public. Her strong assertion against Beijing's actions, and what she saw as its betrayal of promises to respect the city's autonomy in accordance with the principle of 'One Country, Two Systems', struck a chord amongst Taiwanese. In a statement in June 2019, she said that the 'protests in Hong Kong not only made Taiwanese cherish their existing democratic system and way of life even more, but also made it clear to them that the "one country, two systems" [*sic*] model is not viable'.[6]

By the time Tsai started her campaign for re-election, her greatest electoral asset was her clear critical stance on Xi's China. Since the DPP had returned to power in 2016, Beijing had replaced its previous hard–soft strategy with one that was unambiguously hard. The little space allowed Taiwan internationally through observer status at bodies such as the World

Health Assembly from 2009 was once more closed off. China ended its Hu-era truce on aggressively trying to win over the allegiance of Taiwan's few diplomatic allies by gaining the diplomatic recognition of Panama in 2017 and Nicaragua in 2021. The former was a particularly bitter blow, as Panama was one of Taiwan's longest-standing and most stable partners. After Nicaragua switched its loyalties, only Paraguay was left as the one country in Latin America with formal ties to Taiwan. Once, the continent had been where Taiwan's connections were strongest. But the hardening position of Xi's Beijing earned sympathetic support for Tsai.

Tsai's other great advantage in 2020 was the Nationalist Party itself. Beset by internal problems, it chose as its presidential candidate Han Kuo-yu, a Trump-like controversialist and populist with the significant defect of not being that popular. Despite riding high with his victory in the mayoral election of Kaohsiung in 2018, when opposition to Tsai and the DPP was at its peak, Han was unable to duplicate his success at national level. His antics on the campaign trail saw him make a series of outlandish promises: to double the number of tourists to the island from 11 million a year to 20 million; digitize the 700,000 artefacts in the National Palace Museum; and fund a free year abroad for every Taiwanese student. All of them were easily proven to be unworkable and too expensive, and each in turn was quickly retracted.[7] These blunders were supplemented by Han's habit of speaking more warmly about the Beijing government than the DPP did – a posture on mainland affairs that the media painted as close to capitulation. His visits to Hong Kong and Macau in 2019 occurred against the backdrop of the quarrel over legal jurisdictions mentioned above, which offered the worst kind of advert for what Taiwan's fate might be under a 'One Country, Two Systems' deal. Cautious and considered,

Tsai became an increasingly attractive option for a nervous and risk-averse electorate.

Tsai's victory in 2020 was remarkable because it overturned the negative outcome of the disastrous midterm local elections in 2018. Then, the DPP had lost a large swathe of city and county seats to the opposition, forcing Tsai to resign her chairmanship of the party and striking 'a significant blow to her prospects for re-election', as one report at the time stated.[8] Now, she won 57 per cent of the vote. The DPP also kept control of the Legislative Assembly – which it had won for the first time ever in 2016 – although its share of the chamber's 113 seats fell by seven, to sixty-one. These results were recognition that Tsai had managed to balance an almost impossible and explosive combination of demands successfully, and that she deserved a second term.

During Tsai's second stint as president, America has added to her difficulties. The shift from the Trump presidency to the Biden administration – with Trump's more isolationist 'America First' attitude giving way to Biden's more multilateralist, outward-looking diplomacy – has made US policy hard to predict. Nevertheless, up to 2024 Tsai managed the fluctuating international environment and Taiwan's domestic challenges with deftness and skill, showing herself to be a remarkable statesperson and one of the most noteworthy international leaders of her time.

The Voice of Taiwanese People

Where is Taiwanese democracy after the long and winding road it has travelled up to 2024? We know well enough what elite leaders such as the four above think, because they have said so much and are so well recorded. But what about ordinary Taiwanese people? What are their views on all this? Elections produce a lot of information in terms of who votes, and whom they vote for, and about what public opinion is on key political issues in Taiwan. This provides something that no one has access to in China, not even its seemingly all-powerful leaders. For the People's Republic of China, any claims about what the public feels or believes remain largely suppositions. No election data can be produced to prove where people's thoughts might really lie, nor is extensive public surveying allowed, or the expression of contentious or alternative views within the media. Even social media remains highly controlled and censored. With Taiwan, it is the complete opposite. There is not just the bald quantitative data from elections, but also endless surveying delivering a plethora of different qualitative data and information. In this way, we can at least gain a little insight into the hearts and minds of ordinary people.

What they clearly show in the years since 1996 is two things. First, on the specific all-important matter of cross-strait relations, most evidence has consistently shown support for maintaining the current status quo, either permanently or for the time being, with no desire for confrontation.[9] Those that adopt more assertive policies, either pro- or anti-engagement with China, tend not to garner lots of votes. This is a prudent, cautious electorate. It has tended to want leaders who did not take risks, while at the same time making sure Taiwan was well defended and fairly treated by the outside world. The second clear strand is constant concerns about the economy and standards of living. That explains why Taiwanese don't mind trade connections cross-strait, as long as they bring benefits (thus the initial strong support for Ma Ying-jeou, because his policies were viewed as trying to achieve this). They do mind Taiwan being humiliated and belittled on the international stage. And they certainly reject the current option of 'One Country, Two Systems', with 90 per cent in 2020 saying no to it.[10] They are able to joke about the ban on Taiwanese pineapples by the mainland after political squabbles in 2021. But they also appreciate the solidarity that Japan showed in mounting a campaign to buy the fruit China had rejected.[11]

Things are changing, however. Taiwanese public opinion on China has hardened since Tsai came to power in 2016. The numbers of those saying they wanted no discussions of unification even under the loosest terms has increased. One survey even showed that more than half the population supported an eventual move to independence, rising from a third a few years before.[12] Those who express distrust and suspicion of China are in the majority now. Some critics domestically and in the US are concerned that Taiwanese are almost too nonchalant about the threat of Chinese attack. Spending on defence has remained stagnant in Taiwan, in some areas decreasing since 2000, before modest rises in 2023.[13] The national service requirements have dwindled almost to the point that they are no longer functional, though recent reforms have tried to address this with a restoration of one-year compulsory conscription in 2024.[14] Many feel that Taiwan is overly dependent on its defensive alliance with the US, which supplies the air force's main fighter jet (the F-16), along with a large variety of other high-tech military equipment, from ballistic missiles to radar. The vulnerability of Taiwan's position in this situation is underlined by the fact that these supplies are not guaranteed by any formal treaty agreements, but occur through informal, unwritten understandings framed by the loose commitments of the 1979 Act of Congress. They can be interrupted (and in the past have been) due to the US not wanting to antagonize China against its own interests. The most famous example of this was in 1982, when President Ronald Reagan undertook to reduce the sale of military technology to the island.

For outsiders, Taiwanese politics bears a superficial resemblance to the politics in Europe or America. The fact that there are opposing parties on the island suggests they occupy a spectrum, running from left to right. But the DPP and Nationalists, along with a host of smaller parties around them, don't fall into such easy categories.[15] There are policies the DPP has adopted in the past, from anti-immigration platforms to strong support for business, that might belong better to right-wing entities elsewhere. But the DPP has also been supportive of liberal positions on same-sex marriages, and union rights, putting it firmly in the progressive camp. Its policy mix doesn't conform to a Western model.

The Nationalists too are variable, sometimes embracing heavy state involvement in and support of the economy, then lining up with progressive measures such as liberalization of the educational curriculum. Even on mainland policy, once the area of their sharpest disagreements with their main opponents, they have tended to shift their position, moving from the softer line of the Ma era to a far harder approach in 2024, albeit one that still encouraged contact and dialogue.

Whatever differences recent surveys have shown about social, economic and political issues, the resistance to closer alignment with China is – in a situation full of nuance and ambiguity – starkly unambiguous. The notion of reunification, or unification, is one that Taiwanese people do not support. Beijing surely knows this. There are issues over what sort of information gets through the iron wall of advisors and gatekeepers around Xi Jinping, and whether he has any access to data that conveys such unwelcome messages. But whatever the final outcome of the current cross-strait situation, any outsiders – whether China or anyone else – who attempt to impose one on the island need to reckon with the depth of public feeling in Taiwan. Physical conquest would be hard enough. Overcoming the barriers in people's hearts and minds looks insurmountable.

This crucial point has always been understood by observers and analysts. Richard Bush, a former State Department official from the US who wrote about potential solutions in the 2000s, emphasized one crucial fact: whatever might be decided to settle Taiwan's future, it would need democratic validation by the population on the island.[16] And for China, even if it tried to enforce what it desires, it would have to manage profound opposition from the Taiwanese. A conquering China would end up trying to govern a Taiwan where the population was united against it, resentful and rebellious. Managing this situation politically and economically would sap even Beijing's vast resources. It would also be out of character for a country that has largely shown itself to be risk averse and to prefer stability over adventurism in its foreign relations.

2024

The morning of election day, 13 January, was beautifully clear and sunny in Taipei. As I walked along the streets, there was a still, hushed air of anticipation. The months of arguments, rallies, debates and heated exchanges between the competing parties were over. Finally, by the end of the day, there would be a result. One of the three figures fighting for the position would prevail. Taiwan would have a new president.

After all the recent tumult, the polling stations that day were havens of calm. One I passed was in a family temple. Those voting could do so with the smell of orchids and incense in the air. Another was beside an administrative building. A notice stuck on the pavement near to the door stated that no canvassing or political activity or attempt to interfere with those trying to vote could happen within thirty metres of the polling station itself. By four in the afternoon, the business of unsealing the ballot boxes and then preparing to count their contents was underway.

That the incumbent DPP's candidate, William Lai Ching-te, managed to come through in the end with a reasonably sized majority (40 per cent of the total vote) belied the underlying message of the campaign. The electorate was split, and the fact that Lai was able to clinch victory on just over two fifths of the turnout was symptomatic of that. The young in particular, many of them wandering around in the distinctive white campaigning clothes of the TPP, had come out in force for Ko Wen-je's new party. They expressed deep antipathy to the older, better-established parties. Ko's concern about the huge costs of living, and the ways that inflation had eaten away at whatever wage rises had happened in the last few years, struck a deep chord with those under the age of thirty who had yet to fully establish their careers or get on the property ladder. One first-time voter told me how upset their parents were at their intention to vote for Ko. But they found it impossible to contemplate choosing either the DPP or the Nationalist Party.

Still, change was definitely in the air. Chinese diplomats made predictably fierce comments about what they regarded as an inappropriate and misguided outcome. 'Taiwan is China's Taiwan,' Chen Binhua, an official of the State Council in Beijing, asserted after the result was announced. 'This election cannot change the basic pattern and the development of cross-Strait relations, nor can it change the common desire of compatriots on both sides of the Taiwan Strait to draw closer,' he continued.[17] But the fact that Lai won by as wide a margin as he did showed that the differences between China and the island had never been greater, and that all the indicators were that they would only increase.

The issue of relations with China had invariably woven its way in and out of the campaign, proving the most challenging topic for all of the candidates. Lai had to explain as a slip of the tongue a remark he had made in the presidential debate about the need to strike the words 'Republic of China' from the constitution and replace them with 'Taiwan' – an action Beijing would certainly regard as a de facto declaration of independence and would take action against. Hou Yu-yi of the Nationalist Party had to give similarly painstaking reassurances that there would be no talks on unification with the mainland under his stewardship. Both he and Ko, however, did support more dialogue with China. The final election result showed an almost equal split in attitudes, with as many people voting for parties advocating a softer approach to mainland issues as those who supported a harder line.

The 2024 election did what democracy does best – lay out in the open the reality of public opinion, which politicians then need to address, no matter how complex the picture that has been painted. Lai's victory handed him arguably the most unenviable and difficult job on the planet. He had a divided population, the majority of whom had not voted for him, and a divided world, with China facing off against the US. Somehow he would have to bridge these chasms around him.

4. The Role of Taiwan's Economy and the Superconductors That Power Global Information Technology

Hsinchu Science Park, southwest of Taipei, is not a scenic spot for tourists to wander around. But on days when the temperature is not so searing that it melts the soles of your shoes and drenches you in sweat if you step outside, or when there are no torrential rains or typhoons to send you scuttling back into the welcome shelter of a taxi, it has a certain kind of serene calm.

A complex of severe and massive buildings rears up either side of a bisecting road, behind a small boundary of trees, grass and foliage. There are tiny wooden statues peering out: a frog fishing in a small pond, a line of cartoonish rabbits gazing at passers-by. A sign invites pedestrians to follow the 'green route' between the Morris Chang Building and the vast factory next to it. But the path leads somewhat unpromisingly into what appears to be a maze of concrete. And security guards are watching, clearly a little intrigued by why someone should be wandering around so leisurely while everyone else has a purposeful stride, on their way to somewhere else.

Science parks like Hsinchu are dotted across the world. They have a certain generic feel, with their box-like buildings mass-producing whatever they do to fill the global markets with goods. But this particular spot has an elevated status, something it acquired long after it was established in 1980 to pilot a new kind of economic strategy, one where the government invested and private enterprise innovated. Debate rages to this day about exactly what further role the state played, and what can be attributed to other factors. But one thing is indisputable: in 1987, this science park backed one particular winner. That windowless white monolith and the dark glass-clad block abutting it contain one of the world's most valuable companies, one responsible for 8 per cent of Taiwan's overall economic output, and 12 per cent of its exports. More than that, this place sits at the centre of the global economy, a beating heart that pumps out the chips and semiconductors that power everything from coffee makers and drones, to smartphones and artificial intelligence systems. You may not know it, but you are more than likely to be carrying around one of those chips right now in your pocket.

By 2023, the Taiwan Semiconductor Manufacturing Company (TSMC) produced over 90 per cent of the world's most advanced semiconductors, the critical components that power every computer. Without them – 'the brains of modern electronics' – 'there would be no smartphones, radios, TVs, computers, video games, or advanced medical diagnostic equipment'.[1] The early phase of the COVID-19 pandemic in 2020, the trade wars between the US and China, the Russian invasion of Ukraine in early 2022, and finally bad weather in Taiwan itself in 2021 all caused massive disruption in the supply of these critical components of the modern economy.[2] It was a small taste of what might happen were TSMC to cease functioning.

Were this a geopolitical thriller, the addition of this factor to the already complicated cross-strait situation would be regarded as a plot twist too far. For the dispute between China and Taiwan is not just a geopolitical matter, but a geoeconomic one too. Taiwan ranked fourteenth globally in terms of GDP in 2022.[3] According to *Global Finance* magazine's 2023 ratings, in terms of per capita GDP adjusted for purchasing power parity,

Taiwan was wealthier than most major European states, apart from Switzerland, Norway, Ireland and Denmark.[4] But above and beyond raw baseline data, there was what some called 'the silicon shield'. For the amazing fact was that if the rest of the world relied on getting its high-tech semiconductors from Taiwan, that included China. Indeed, despite many attempts to catch up, China was even more dependent than others. It was the largest manufacturer of electronic goods in the world. And, for many of them, components sourced from its neighbour across the strait were crucial.

The 'semiconductor wars', as they have come to be called, are a distinct but hugely significant element of the Taiwan–China conundrum. It would be tempting to say that this was all in accordance with a deliberate strategic plan on Taiwan's part. But in the early phase of Taiwan's economic development, the aim was merely to be more self-sufficient, and to become a little bit wealthier. The day Hsinchu Science Park was founded, there were no neat blueprints for how economic success would have important national security implications. That was all to unfold later.

Fighting to be Rich: The Early Years

The start was not auspicious. After the Nationalist creation of a separate government on the island in the late 1940s, there was precious little advanced industry. What did exist was the result of half a century of Japanese rule. Reasonable infrastructure was in place, with rail, road and functioning ports. War had not decimated this the way it had on the mainland, where the situation was far worse. But, for all its challenges, Taiwan was perhaps the wealthiest and best developed part of the Republic

of China before 1949 and contained the seeds for its later transformation. The question was what would encourage this now
the new rulers had nowhere else to govern and could concen-
trate solely on the small territory they had clung on to.

As mentioned before, Chiang Kai-shek's track record was
hardly one to inspire much confidence in terms of economic
performance. His final phase in charge of greater China had
been chaotic, inflicting inflation and rampant corruption on
almost every level of the economy. It had been enough to alienate the US and build public support for the more frugal and
disciplined Communists. But on Taiwan, things were easier to
control. And there was the great advantage until the mid-1960s
of US aid. That was invested in creating the initial platform for
more manufacturing and industry. There was also a pool of
well-educated cheap labour. Chiang's government helped
things by implementing a series of land reforms addressing
some of the social imbalances and inequalities on the island.
From 1949, rents were capped, tenants were allowed to buy
public land, and large estates were finally split up and sold off
to individual buyers. This was partly achieved through American assistance. But it created a far more competitive and
efficient agricultural sector. And it did this with none of the
violence and long-term political bad feeling that the same process created on the mainland. Over the Chiang years, the
Taiwanese economy steadily improved.

By the 1970s, Taiwan had become one of the Four Asian
Tigers of the region (the others were Hong Kong, Singapore
and South Korea). In concert with Japan and South Korea, it
had entered the global economy by manufacturing and exporting goods and components that had become too expensive, or
too polluting, to make elsewhere. The markets of Europe and
North America were the chief destination for the things it

made. Taiwan's agriculture sector remained important, but in a country where most land was mountainous and unusable, high-value production was the key to future wealth creation.

The great shift in economic policy occurred under Chiang's successor – his son Ching-kuo. From 1976, the so-called 'Ten Major Construction Projects' began. Of these, the most prominent was the new international airport in Taoyuan, near the capital, as well as ports, highways and steel mills. During the 1960s and 1970s, growth reached 10 per cent annually.[5] But by the 1980s, after the creation of over 160 universities or colleges of further education, Taiwan was ready for what was called the decade of its 'miracle'. Throughout the 1980s and 1990s, Taiwan's economy grew at more than 7 per cent a year. Although a lower percentage than before, it occurred in a much larger economy, producing far greater and more sustained outcomes. Government plans set out aspirations to become a major fibre producer for clothing and fabrics (by 1989, Taiwan's sector was the second largest in the world, after Japan). Buying technology from American and Japanese companies, the island established a major consumer electronics sector. Another significant development was that by the middle of the 2000s, services made up more than half of the economy, fundamentally changing its structure. A poor country which barely registered less than half a century before was now a powerhouse.

State Supporter

The role the island's government played in Taiwan's economic development is a hotly debated question. Some view its input as crucial; others see a far more organic and complex relationship between it and other actors. Foreign partnership, particularly with the US and Japan, was clearly important. So too were the Taiwanese from the 1950s onwards who studied in the US and then, after careers abroad, decided to return to their homeland and work there. Of these, Morris Chang, the founder of TSMC, is the best known and perhaps the most significant.

Certainly the role of what one political scientist has called the 'Taiwanese technocratic . . . bureaucracy' – the officials at national and local level who set out the policies to support economic development – was crucial.[6] Globalization helped, creating access to new markets where Taiwanese products could be sold.[7] The outcomes from this cooperation between government and business on the island had more than just economic results. 'The Taiwanese IT industry,' the same scholar explained, 'has been shaped by its formal international political isolation', with the island's capacity and influence in this field a crucial means of building at least one bridge to the outside world.[8] Economic issues were never just about wealth and the material betterment of daily lives, but had to figure as part of a security strategy. 'As in many developing countries today,' another study argues, 'the Taiwanese rulers had to consider their [economic policy's] potential for exacerbating or mitigating domestic . . . foreign security problems.'[9] So the state had a clear role, even if a very different one from the companies and other entities involved, in viewing things in this larger and broader context. More practically too, it supplied support in terms of capital, tax breaks and other preferential policies, and often acted as one of the chief customers. But it had to have winners to back, and that was largely the work of happenstance, experimentation and creativity by non-state actors.

Semiconductors offer a classic case study of how this process worked. In the beginning, during the 1970s, the Taiwanese government's science and technology administration did not see this sector as a viable one. It was too capital intensive, demanding high levels of investment and financial support. The country did not possess the key technology, and therefore either needed to procure it from elsewhere or put significant resources into research and development to try to create it. There was inevitable reluctance by officials to considering entering an arena where the Japanese, Dutch and Americans seemed well ahead and would do everything they could to prevent competition.[10]

Morris Chang was a key player in changing this situation, which was to have momentous consequences. Born in China in 1931, into a middle-class family, he left during the Communist takeover at the age of eighteen. In an interview in 2007, he recalled how 'China was so poor, most of the people were so poor, even [the] middle class'.[11] The US, where he moved, 'was a paradise when I first arrived', because of its social, political and educational advancement. Studying at Harvard and the Massachusetts Institute of Technology, he initially failed to be accepted on to a doctoral programme, so went to work for Texas Instruments, an American information technology company. Only while there did he manage to complete a doctorate. A quarter of a century of service to the company ended in the early 1980s with no new job lined up. But Chang had the rare combination of management skills and technological knowledge, which made him an attractive proposition for other companies and partners. It was understandable why Li Kwoh-ting, Minister without Portfolio in the Chiang Ching-kuo administration in the 1980s, targeted Chang. Li was a talent spotter; seeing the Chinese American at a loose end, he was an obvious figure to recruit. The new ethos in Taiwan took semiconductors seriously, and Chang seemed the perfect man to deliver something.

Chang admitted that on his initial retirement, while reasonably well off, he was not by any means a wealthy man. Whatever the financial inducements may have been, his move to Taiwan in 1985 was motivated as much by a desire to take an 'opportunity to make some money personally' as it was by the wish to assist in strengthening Taiwan's economic capacity. He also acknowledged that the support of government, along with important investment from the Dutch company Philips and an active technology-transfer programme in operation at the time (whereby the exchange of certain kinds of intellectual property was encouraged between countries), greatly helped him in the task he had set himself. Chang knew after three decades in the high-tech and semiconductor industry how fiercely competitive it was. Whatever Taiwan did, it was up against major American, Japanese and European corporations. 'We had no strength in research and development, or very little anyway,' Chang said in 2007. 'We had no strength in circuit design, IC product design,' he continued, referring to the integrated circuits that are a key component of semiconductors. 'We had little strength in sales and marketing, and we had almost no strength in intellectual property. The only possible strength that Taiwan had, and even that was a potential one . . . was semiconductor manufacturing, wafer manufacturing.'

In the Museum of Innovation at TSMC in Hsinchu, located next to the building named after Chang today, there is an electronic copy of the first business plan he presented to the Taiwanese government, in 1987. It makes the case for what he wanted to do in very simple terms. There were four parts to the process of making semiconductors, as he saw it. First of all was development: IC board design, and planning what needed to be made and why. Second was creating the technology to bring these products into existence. Third was the actual manufacturing of them. Finally, they needed to be sold to customers. Companies tended to try to do all of these stages. They'd come up with an idea, then have to invest in the means of making it, go through the production process, and after that do the selling. But as technology advanced, it became clear that the levels of investment, and the ever-increasing specialization, meant it was harder and harder to do everything in-house.

Chang's proposal was that TSMC focus only on the second and third parts of the process (designing the machines to make the products and then manufacturing the chips). Its customers would be companies with an idea for a chip and what it could be used for. They'd bring that to Chang's new venture, and agree on the best way of manufacturing it. TSMC then simply produced the chips for their client, who went on to use them for whatever requirement they had (usually as part of laptops, smartphones, robots or other products). It did not deal with sales to end users such as consumers or smaller retailers; there are no TSMC-branded goods in the world. And yet most homes probably have products with key components in them made by the company. Opting out of the first and final stages meant that massive focus was placed on producing the best processes and equipment for making chips and only chips.

Employing this model over the next two decades, Chang created a phenomenally successful company. It was one that was not just reliant on high levels of research and development, and massive capital investment, but on a specific culture. The most important thing TSMC needed was trust from those who used it. It needed customers to entrust it with their ideas and their innovations, secure in the belief that these would never be copied or duplicated. The company was able to do this because it opted out of the business of selling directly to consumers, instead making money solely from the client who had come to it with the design idea in the first place. These were usually manufacturers of other parts of the product, who simply needed semiconductor technology rather than anything else.

When you visit the factory, it is easy to see just what a challenge it is meeting the demands of this very specialist market. The sheer level of technology needed to make these products, and the massive amounts of capital and technical knowledge required, are astounding. A camera shows different parts of the chip-manufacturing process. Standing gazing at it all, I was overcome by the sheer complexity of what was involved. Humans barely appeared on the factory floor. Almost impossible levels of cleanliness are required. Suspended from electronic rails on the ceiling, small robotic machines ran with an eerie, almost human purposefulness, sporadically dropping components down on extendable wires in order to add to whatever product was being made. These buildings, which are so simple and featureless on the outside, inside are a symphony of activity and constantly moving parts.

The relentless focus on being just a chipmaker meant that TSMC has been continuously profitable from 1991. By May 2024, it had become the ninth most valuable company in the world, with a market capitalization of US$730 billion.[12] In little more than a decade, it had increased its value tenfold. Chang served as the chief executive officer until 2005, and then a second time from 2009 to his full retirement in 2018. A self-effacing man, in an interview with the *New York Times* in 2023, then well into his nineties, he said that 'I would rather stay relatively unknown'. At the same time, he showed a clear awareness of what his contribution had brought to Taiwan. 'I was literally sure that we had achieved technology leadership . . . I don't think we'll lose it.'[13]

Chang was also a major player in creating something that China clearly wanted. 'We control all the choke points,' he told the *New York Times*. 'China can't really do anything if we want to choke them.' Its dependence on TSMC technology is still high, despite many efforts to accelerate the growth of its indigenous industry. The problems, however, are as much technical as political. The semiconductor business is partly a race to the most miniature. The precision needed to produce the most advanced chips is staggering. So too are the supply chains. TSMC may be one principal source of the industry's best products. But it is dependent on an ecosystem where just one of the most advanced lasers used for producing the chips itself requires 457,329 separate components.[14] Building up the sort of supply chains that can satisfy this complexity is the work of decades, not days. In addition, the manufacturing process's need for large amounts of readily available pure water means that, geographically speaking, Taiwan is one of the best-situated places for the industry. Despite vast research and development funding, China still lags Taiwan by a decade or more. It seems to be perpetually chasing a mirage, its object forever receding from it.

Just how much of a security guarantee is this for the island? On that point, there is disagreement. According to one report, 'When it comes to semiconductors, China needs Taiwan more than the other way around.'[15] But another perspective is simply that the presence of this incredibly valuable and important technology in a territory that China regards as its own only makes Beijing more anxious to take the island. 'In the current scenario, TSMC's position makes China covet Taiwan even more,' Wu Jieh-min at the Taiwanese research institute Academia Sinica was quoted as saying.[16] This is particularly so in view of the increased US investment in producing top-quality

semiconductors back home. For all the talk by Taiwanese officials of the 'silicon shield' protecting them, reliance on it as an
absolute guarantee of the island's safety and security would be
foolhardy. After all, an attack by China would not only smash
its own source of supply but also those of everyone else. Lose-
lose this might be; but in Beijing's eyes, at least, it doesn't cede
any advantages to its competitors.

What the presence of TSMC *does* do is complicate an
already complex situation. The scenario planners in foreign
governments and international organizations need to factor
into the mix not just the military and geopolitical fallout of
conflict between China and Taiwan, but also the absolute certainty that it will wreak havoc on the global economy, if only
because of the collapse in supply of this one profoundly
important component. Morris Chang betrayed the calm dis-
position that allowed him to be such an effective scientist and
business person when, speaking in 2023, he said that 'the chance
of China invading Taiwan, amphibious warfare and all that
stuff, I think that's a very, very low probability'. Even a blockade of some kind he considered a 'low probability', although
'it's still a chance and I want to avoid that'.[17] We have to hope
that, just as Chang was right in the 1980s when speaking to the
Taiwanese government about backing his ideas for semiconductors and building a whole industry, he is right on this too.

Foxconn: A Taiwanese Company Getting Rich in China

Few knew, when the Hon Hai Precision Tool Company was
established in Taipei in 1974, that it would one day produce
almost half of the world's consumer electronic products. If
someone has an Apple iPhone, a Sony television or a Nintendo

gaming system, then the likelihood is that Foxconn is part of their lives, whether they are aware of it or not.

Foxconn is a good counterexample to set against TSMC. Both companies were closely linked with visionary, tough-minded founders. The man who set up Foxconn, Terry Gou, has a story every bit as dramatic as Morris Chang's. He was born in Taipei in 1950, a year after the Communist victory on the mainland, to parents from central Shaanxi province who fought in the Nationalist army. Gou had a humble upbringing, working in a rubber factory at a grinding wheel after graduation from school and college. The company he founded in the early seventies with only US$7,500 began by making plastic components for television sets in a small rented shed in a suburb of Taipei. By the 1980s, it had gained contracts from the Japanese company Atari to manufacture parts for their gaming kits. But the big time came when the Chinese market opened up.

Gou is someone who associates closely with China. In 2023, he even stood for the Taiwanese presidency, saying that he did not want the island to become another Ukraine, suffering invasion by its neighbour, and that he would bring it 'back from the abyss of war with China'.[18] He has reason to fear conflict more than most. From 1988, the company he founded has done most of its manufacturing in places such as Shenzhen, just opposite Hong Kong, and Zhengzhou, in the central province of Henan. These production hubs are more like cities than factories, employing up to 450,000 people in Shenzhen and 250,000 in Zhengzhou. Having cashed in on the plentiful supply of cheap and well-educated labour in the early years, by the 2000s Gou's mainland factories were producing most of the world's iPhones. Many Chinese became addicted to these foreign-branded products. The dissident Liu Xiaobo said that God had bestowed the internet on China as a 'universal grace . . . extended to all Chinese in our suffering'.[19] Terry Gou played a major role in supplying most of the smartphones by which Chinese today access its benefits. This business alone made him a billionaire.

While Foxconn is one of the great contemporary symbols of cross-strait collaboration, representing the ways in which China and Taiwan are now deeply interconnected and inter-linked with each other, it also provides a lot of lessons about the perils of such intimacy. A spate of suicides by workers at Foxconn's Longhua Shenzhen complex in 2010 raised questions about just how great the opportunity to work for an advanced high-tech company was for young Chinese. Migrants, largely from the countryside, had become the foot soldiers of the eco-nomic revolution in the era after 1980. But they lived precarious and hard lives, often working eighteen-hour days, sometimes in conditions of Dickensian harshness.

On the surface, Longhua was one of the best places to work in China. Gyms, swimming pools, decent dormitories and a clean environment are what the visitor sees, and what the com-pany is keen to promote as part of its image. But insider accounts told of a draconian work culture, swift and brutal treatment of any hints of protest, and a slew of mental-health problems that grew into a widespread crisis. In the 2010 inci-dent, workers started to throw themselves from the top of buildings. An estimated eighteen such attempts were made that year, with fourteen resulting in death. One man working at the factory was quoted in a report in 2017 saying, 'It wouldn't be Foxconn without people dying. Every year people kill them-selves. They take it as a normal thing.'[20] With up to twelve people to a tiny dorm, and some processing 1,700 iPhones in a twelve-hour workday, it is easy to see why depression set in. Employees interviewed secretly painted 'a bleak picture of a high-pressure working environment where exploitation is routine and where depression and suicide have become normalised'.

Gou himself bowed and apologized at a press conference when these deaths became international news. Saying that he did not run a sweatshop, he went on to promise that he and his company would 'leave no stone unturned and . . . make sure to find a way to reduce these suicide tendencies'.[21] He vowed to journalists accompanying him on a site tour that 'we can be a better company'. In some ways, however, he was not master of his own enterprise's fate. Foxconn was embedded in the whole context of rapid industrialization and fast-paced progress in China. Social discontent was rising *because* of inequality across the country, not just in Foxconn's vast plants. They were merely a microcosm of far larger forces at work – and ones that, because of their 'foreign' ownership, attracted more scrutiny than others.

Gou weathered this storm. Conditions improved, at least in so far as the wave of suicides was stemmed. But his situation typified that of the many entrepreneurs whose businesses now involved close engagement with China. The 1990s saw the start of the 'Taishang' phenomenon of Taiwanese business people in mainland China ('Tai' stands for 'Taiwan', and 'shang' is Chinese for 'business'). According to analysis by Lee Chun-yi, who did field research interviewing this group in the 2000s, Taishang lived life balancing on a tightrope. Making money and developing their businesses in China, they were granted favourable treatment as the owners of external enterprises. But they were expected to declare their support for the reunification programme of the Chinese government, and to live under the umbrella of the 'one China, one family' ethos, which emphasized the common cultural and ethnic bonds across the strait. More than many others, these people really did have to develop two personalities: one maintaining their relationship with the officials and the partners in China that mattered to their interests there; and one back in Taiwan, where they had to ensure their own government – or the public – didn't read them as quislings and a security threat.[22]

Gou's own attempt to resolve this quandary was to pin his colours to the mast. At the age of seventy-two, he declared he would be standing as an independent candidate in the 2024 presidential election. 'I implore the people of Taiwan to give me four years,' he boomed at the press conference announcing his candidature on 28 August 2023. 'I promise that I will bring peace to the Taiwan Strait for the next fifty years and lay the deepest foundation of mutual trust between the two sides.' But even at this point, he was forced on the defensive, having to answer embarrassing questions about his links to China and deny that he had ever been 'under the control' of the Communist Party.[23]

Gou's insertion of himself into an already crowded field threatened to splinter a divided electorate further. Facing the incumbent DPP, and the main opposition party, the Nationalists, he also posed a threat to the new emerging force, the Taiwan People's Party. A four-way split, when first past the post won the election, raised the possibility of someone triumphing with the support of a quarter of the electorate, or even less – hardly a compelling mandate by which to govern. For some, though, Gou offered the kind of disruptive challenge to a complacent system and entrenched self-interest that Trump had served up a few years earlier in the US. Gou was a firm supporter of the One China principle, preserving the status quo while aiming for eventual peaceful reunification when both sides agreed. The erosion of public support for these views over the previous years had clearly worried him. One survey showed that 70 per cent of Taiwanese disagreed with his assessment. Their view of Beijing was that it was far more antagonistic and threatening.[24]

The question Gou raised was just how sensible the continuation of a confrontational view towards China was. Ambiguity and cautiousness had served to prevent at least the escalation of the crisis for the last seventy years. And the fact was that, despite the dimming of views about China, polling in 2023 showed a majority of people supported parties with a more conciliatory view towards the mainland and a desire for some level of political contact. While people didn't like the way Beijing spoke to them, nor did they necessarily want to shout back and get into a fight.

As he had been with his business, Gou was now being buffeted by forces more powerful than even a formidable operator such as he could control. In late October 2023, authorities on the mainland revealed that Foxconn's tax affairs were being investigated. Gou had stepped down as Foxconn chief in 2019, but his connection with the company was unavoidable. And in the Chinese state media, scholars associated with Xiamen University's think tank specializing in cross-strait issues spelled out, at least indirectly, the possible political reasons behind the investigations into Gou's affairs by mainland authorities. Ever quick to spot a conspiracy against mainland interests, one of the think tank's researchers, Zhang Wensheng, wrote that 'Gou's announcement of his candidacy will make it even more difficult for non-Green camp to integrate' (green is the colour of the DPP and its allies, who are more independence-leaning). 'The Green camp, especially the "independence faction" forces cheered,' Zhang continued, 'and even called on Green camp supporters to join the election campaign for Gou.'[25] Such an outcome – a split between those merely keener on greater contact with China and those with a strong One China attitude – was one way in which the DPP could pull through and win. Gou read the message of the tax investigation clearly enough. On 24 November he announced that he was 'withdrawing his body, but not his spirit' from the race.[26]

Searching for Economic Alternatives: The New Southbound Policy

It's a common headache across the Pacific, and increasingly in the rest of the world these days: how to maintain balance when your biggest trade and economic partner is China and your major security guarantor is the US? One hundred and twenty countries now name China as their main trading partner.[27] And yet the People's Republic, in the East and Southeast Asia region and elsewhere, has ambitions that unsettle and worry most of those countries.

Of all the tectonic fault lines on which Taiwan sits, this economic quandary is the most important. It is the one that much of the outside world can most relate to, because it is in the same position. Taiwanese are at the forefront of handling this novel situation. Once upon a time, serendipitously, America filled the roles of both chief trading partner and security ally. But that era is over. Taiwan now is engaged in the same business as other countries of seeking diversification in order to mitigate the risks of economic overdependence on China. Even though, as Foxconn and TSMC vividly illustrate, China is where it still continues to generate much of its wealth and a great deal of its business.

In the 2020s, everyone has their plan B. For Europeans and Americans, it is the Indo-Pacific, a concept which assumes that China can be 'contained', 'managed' and 'pushed back against'. Plenty are sceptical about how coherent this idea really is. India, a key element of this strategy, is hardly a natural ally of the West, due to its close relationship with Russia and its increasingly nationalistic turn under Prime Minister Narendra Modi since 2014, despite being a democracy. And within the region, the embrace of forms of multilateralism where countries seek the sort of tighter alliance that the European Union best illustrates is lukewarm. China has come up with its massive Belt and Road Initiative, an attempt to operate on its own terms away from what it regards as the US's constant prying and attempts to interfere, by offering aid, incentives and preferential treatment for infrastructure projects across the region originated by the People's Republic.

Taiwan's own solution to the economic conundrum is the New Southbound Policy (NSP). An attempt to strengthen the island's links with partners such as South Korea, Japan, Indonesia, Malaysia and India, the NSP was put on hold in the Ma Ying-jeou era, when the default strategy was to lean towards China. But under Tsai Ing-wen it has enjoyed a second burst. In her National Day address in 2017, she said that the aim of the NSP was for Taiwan to 'hold a more advantageous position in international society'.[28] In a modest way, it has achieved this. Taiwan's investments in the ten Association of Southeast Asian Nations (ASEAN) rose 73 per cent from 2015 to 2016. One estimate claims that 10 per cent of Taiwanese investment originally destined for China ended up in other Asian countries in the five years up to 2021. Exports to the region increased a quarter over the same period. Singapore, Vietnam and Thailand all significantly grew their trade with Taiwan. That the island was able to achieve results like these in a relatively short time frame only shows, as one analyst put it, the 'strong element of distrust towards China among Southeast Asian elites'.[29]

India too joined in this new game. Modi, before becoming Prime Minister in 2014, had visited Taiwan as the general secretary of his Bharatiya Janata Party (BJP) in 2011. Taiwan and India have signed a number of bilateral agreements covering science and technology, double taxation, air services and agriculture since then. India also hosted 100 Taiwanese companies by 2022; both Foxconn and TSMC have a presence in the country or a link with Indian partners. In terms of Indian presence in Taiwan, 5,000 Indians now live and work on the island. In the five years from 2017, two-way trade grew by over 60 per cent.[30]

One of the challenges that the NSP addresses is the very low birth rate in Taiwan. Taiwan, like Japan and China, now has an ageing population. People are marrying later, and many are choosing to have one child, or none. As in Western societies, there are more people living alone. Migration is one solution to the problem of how to stop a population stagnating. It is not a popular one in the region. In 2018, there were 700,000 foreign nationals based on the island. According to Digital Minister Audrey Tang, the work permit scheme for highly skilled people managed to attract some of the best brains during the pandemic, particularly from elsewhere in Asia. They admired Taiwan's management of the crisis, and its positive, supportive attitude towards innovative research and development.[31]

Lower down the employment hierarchy, however, things are less straightforward. Migrants from Southeast Asia face many barriers when they move to work in Taiwan. Employees at one factory in 2021 claimed they were detained in their place of work, denied freedom to travel, and subjected to the same kinds of draconian rules as were reportedly seen at Foxconn's China factories. Filipino and Indonesian fishermen in 2019 were found to be living on board their boats because Taiwanese local authorities refused to offer them accommodation. The unsafeness of these conditions was proven when a bridge collapsed on to several vessels, killing six of their crew.[32] Other migrants were found to be working in factories with poor health and safety conditions, splashing toxic chemicals on their skin because of a lack of protective clothing.

On paper, Taiwan has done a lot to address these issues. But compared to the flow of investment and capital, and of goods and services, that of people coming to live, work and even put down permanent roots in Taiwan has not operated so seamlessly. As a society where 95 per cent classify themselves as ethnically Han, there is already a strong sense of majority conformism. Inevitably, those who are non-Chinese are highly visible. Changing attitudes towards foreigners is unlikely to be something that can occur easily, or quickly.

The New Southbound Policy is also a long-term work in progress. Implementing a world order where China doesn't figure prominently in the realm of trade and business is not easy and might be impossible. That is particularly so when China is on your doorstep, and seemingly has a vast market to be accessed – albeit at the clear diplomatic and political price of mostly having to agree with the Chinese position, or risk the consequences. But Taiwan is trying, and it is not alone.

Taiwan's Economic Travails

Issued on World Happiness Day, 20 March, a survey in 2021 claimed that Taiwanese were the happiest people in East Asia.

Assessed on six factors – GDP, life expectancy, generosity, social support, freedom and corruption – in the UN Sustainable Development Solutions Network *World Happiness Report*, Taiwan had risen from forty-second place in 2013 to twenty-fourth eight years later.[33] It is true: never before have Taiwanese lived so long, been so prosperous, and as free and well governed. They have world-class healthcare, strong social security and low amounts of crime and disorder, which all contribute to this happiness.

Despite this, there are plenty of threats to the general levels of contentedness. The ever-present anxiety over cross-strait tensions, and what crisis might suddenly erupt from it, is just one of these. For people's daily lives and sense of prosperity, the period of stellar high growth is now firmly in the past. The 2008 economic crisis hit the island hard, causing a recession before GDP rises returned in 2010. The steep dip in productivity and trade at that time added extra wind to the sails of those lobbying to promote closer links with China. As China's economy boomed, with 10 per cent growth a year between 2008 and 2010, it was hard for other countries battling the impact of the economic crisis to ignore potential opportunities in the People's Republic. And Taiwan had as good a foundation as any to do this from, in view of its geographical closeness and the amount of trade already occurring.

In the 2010s and 2020s, Taiwanese growth has been respectable. From a high of 9 per cent during the initial bounceback from the COVID-19 pandemic in 2021, it averaged 1.4 per cent in 2023.[34] This is the lowest figure since 2009. With rising prices, and spiralling property costs, Taiwanese are likely to feel less secure and less prosperous today than in the previous decade.

On the upside, unemployment is low, staying close to 3 per cent. But wages are also low, and stagnating (even though there have been rises in recent years, these have been eaten away by inflation). People work long hours – the sixth longest, compared to thirty-nine other developed economies in 2022, putting it above the US at ninth.[35] In a survey of workers in 2023, nine out of ten said their earnings were too low, and that they felt they had not seen any significant increases in recent years.[36] Meanwhile, inflation rose in the same year to the highest level for a decade and a half, at 2.5 per cent – still a low level compared to European or other developed countries.[37] All of this contributes to public discontent.

The harsh fact is that despite the attempts to diversify and find opportunities elsewhere, Taiwanese maintain their living standards today in good part because of their economic ties with China. They live in a state of constant paradox where the greatest source of threat to their physical safety is also the single largest guarantor of their material well-being. A possible conflict would therefore tangibly hit the bottom line. This is not just a situation where military issues are dominant; it is also one where, in terms of prosperity, any war or argument with China has immediate consequences. And China, of course, is all too aware of that. As in almost every other dimension when one discusses Taiwan–China relations, with the economy things quickly revert to politics.

5. China's Relations with Taiwan: Friends or Enemies?

On 7 November 2015, in a conference room in the Shangri-La Hotel in Singapore, two men in their sixties met each other for the first time. Only three years separated them in age. Both were born on the mainland, one in central China, one in Hong Kong, then under British colonial rule. Partaking of tea, they politely addressed each other as 'Mister', spending a pleasant couple of hours chatting about life and the world in general.

That this meeting had been possible at all was due to years of hard diplomatic preparation from both sides. The older of the two men, Ma Ying-jeou, was coming to the end of his second and final term as Taiwan's president. The man he was meeting, Xi Jinping, was just three years into what has since become a seemingly perpetual presidency. Leaders of the Chinese Communist Party and the Nationalists had not met since Mao Zedong and Chiang Kai-shek had held a summit just after the end of the Second World War. Leaders of China and Taiwan had never met at all. In every sense, this was a historic occasion. 'No force can pull us apart,' said Xi as the talks opened. 'We are one family.' Ma responded, 'Even though this is the first meeting, we feel like old friends.'[1]

The 2015 rapprochement was a huge move symbolically, but it ended up leading to no long-term dramatic changes. Today, it stands as the high point of a process of alignment which led nowhere. The complicated reasons for this will be spelled out in this chapter. But what is clear is that only a matter of months after Xi and Ma chatted to each other while sipping their tea in the Singapore sunshine things on both sides of the strait changed.

One significant event occurred in Taiwan. Within a year of the meeting, Ma's successor as president, representing the opposition DPP, was voted in by a landslide. Tsai Ing-wen led a party and a government that immediately antagonized the Beijing leadership. Top-level political contact stopped. Tourist numbers soon plummeted as more restrictions were put in place. Between 2016 and 2018, visitors from the mainland holidaying on the island dropped from 4.2 million to 2.7.[2] In 2019, Beijing banned individual travellers from venturing across the strait. While 163,000 Taiwanese lived and worked in China by 2021, this was the eighth year their number had fallen, down from 400,000 in 2011.[3]

An increasing number of those who did stay on the mainland reported feeling discriminated against and harassed. One man working in Shanghai had moved to China in 2006, but was now forced to break up with his long-term girlfriend because her parents – civil servants in the local government – believed his nationality would affect their careers were he to marry their daughter. Another man, who had a young child in a kindergarten in the city, was horrified to hear that at school the children had reportedly been taught to say the slogan, 'We want to destroy the Taiwanese.'[4]

Such stories accompanied the already noted historic rise in negative public opinion towards China amongst the Taiwanese. According to a Pew Research Center survey in 2020, 61 per cent of respondents had unfavourable views of their vast mainland neighbour. Almost half regarded even economic links, until then largely perceived as positive, in a critical light.[5] This was accompanied by shifts in attitude with more overtly political implications. A poll carried out in 2023 revealed that almost half those spoken to wanted to see Taiwanese independence either immediately or at some unspecified point in the future. This marked a four percentage point increase over the previous year, and was the highest level ever recorded. Only 11 per cent supported reunification.[6]

A former Taiwanese official, Jason Hu, was asked by the US journalist Tom Friedman in 1996 what to do about 'the 800-pound gorilla in your living room' and the constant demands of its presence. Hu shot back: 'Tom, it's worse than that. Not only do I have an 800-pound gorilla in my living room, that gorilla happens to think that he's my brother!'[7] Since the mid-2010s, relations with this partner 'that thinks they're your brother' have significantly worsened. This has had a major impact on the security situation cross-strait. When two sides are trying to talk to each other and work their differences out, then the chances of open conflict erupting are reduced a little. But when there is no such contact, and only acrimony, distrust and anger, then it is easy to see how things could quickly fall apart.

As opinions and sentiments in Taiwan have travelled in one direction, so those in China have moved just as fast in the opposite direction. It is as though the more Taiwan wants to be Taiwan, the more strenuously China wants to claim ownership over it. The irony here is that the fastest route for Taiwan to lose what autonomy it currently has would be to state its desire for independence so strongly that China would be forced to act. China remains the great presence sitting in the living room, even if at the moment it is still and inactive. Cross-strait relations are today in a critical situation. At the heart of this lies the attitude both parties have to their relationship with each other, something that has clearly been undergoing profound change in the last few years.

The Chinese Position in Theory

Xi Jinping did not create the Chinese policy on Taiwan, despite criticisms that during his presidency things have deteriorated. In fact, he had very little space for manoeuvre from the moment he came to power. Over the course of his career, there have been a series of top-level statements on Chinese attitudes to cross-strait issues, some of which have elicited a Taiwanese response. The earliest was Ye Jianying's Nine Points, delivered in an interview to the official Xinhua news agency in 1981. Ye was chairman of the Chinese National People's Congress at the time, the Chinese parliament (though one regarded as largely symbolic rather than possessing any operational powers). This was a declaration big on abstract reassurances and promises. It proposed talks between China and Taiwan, the establishment of connections between the two that at the time didn't exist, and the introduction of the 'One Country, Two Systems' idea. After the country was reunified, Ye stated:

> Taiwan can enjoy a high degree of autonomy as a special administrative region and it can retain its armed forces. The Central Government will not interfere with local affairs in Taiwan. Taiwan's current socio-economic system will remain unchanged, so will its way of life and its economic and cultural relations with foreign countries. There will be no encroachment on the proprietary rights and lawful right of inheritance over private property, houses, land and enterprises, or on foreign investments.[8]

Ye's abstractions set the tone for much of what was to follow from Beijing. He also set the precedent of numbered proposals.

Almost a decade and a half later, in 1995, the then-president, Jiang Zemin, issued a follow-up eight-point version. That too encouraged stronger relations and greater trade, basing the logic for reunification on China and Taiwan's shared 5,000 years of culture. It affirmed the idea that, with greater exposure to each other, Taiwanese and Chinese would naturally seek closer ties and, through an almost organic process, become one. 'The historical course of reunifying the motherland is irreversible,' Jiang stated, 'and the continuously developing relation between the two sides of the Taiwan Straits is in accordance with the general trend and the will of the people.'[9] This sounded disarmingly easy.

Exactly a decade afterwards, in 2005, Jiang's successor, Hu Jintao, came out with his own iteration, though it comprised a mere four key points. Perhaps this was due to the fact that, while the issue being addressed had grown no simpler to solve, Chinese certainty about the rightness of their position and the imperative for a road map and time frame for resolution of the status of the island was increasing. The basic premise for Hu was that all attempts at independence or secession would be quashed: 'We will never tolerate "Taiwan independence",' he declared, 'and never allow the "Taiwan independence" secessionist forces to make Taiwan secede from the motherland under any name or by any means.'[10] Evidently goaded by what China believed were the more pro-independence leanings of the Taiwanese president at this time, Chen Shui-bian, an anti-secession law was passed by the Beijing government. It removed any doubt about Chinese intentions by enshrining in law the obligation to use force if Taipei were to declare independence. Four years later, Hu came up with a slightly more emollient six-point proposal, largely encouraging greater economic links and cultural cooperation. This was to accommodate Chen's more amenable successor, Ma Ying-jeou.

Xi Jinping himself has spoken about Taiwan on several occasions since he came to power in 2012. While he has not deployed a numbered list, one China – with Taiwan as part of it – remains the core principle he shares with his predecessors. But he has also talked overtly of a new principle. This is simply that, whereas in the past no timeline was ever mentioned, now the emphasis is on the issue having to be resolved within a finite period. There is acknowledgement of the very different system of governance Taiwan has now, and how challenging it will be to manage this crucial problem. But that is not regarded as an impediment to uniting. 'Different systems are not an obstacle to unification, and even less are they an excuse for separatism,' Xi is reported as stating in 2019. 'The private property, religious beliefs and legitimate rights and interests of Taiwanese compatriots will be fully assured.' If there is not movement towards this vision of unity, 'We make no promise to abandon the use of force, and retain the option of taking all necessary measures.'[11] The mood had palpably changed.

Accompanying such assertions are a trio of White Papers, issued by the Chinese government, and usually regarded as authoritative statements of its policy. The latest of these, published in 2022, contains language typical of the Xi era: 'Resolving the Taiwan question and realizing China's complete reunification is a shared aspiration of all the sons and daughters of the Chinese nation,' the paper declared. 'National rejuvenation has been the greatest dream of the Chinese people and the Chinese nation since the modern era began. Only by realizing complete national reunification can the Chinese people on both sides of the Straits cast aside the shadow of civil war and create and enjoy lasting peace.'[12]

The Chinese position therefore has evolved into something which addresses a complex and sensitive question, one riddled by uncertainty and lack of clarity, with wilfully blind simplicity. The historical record can be dealt with merely by saying that Taiwan has *always* been part of China. That's it; no more questions. The aim is to have reunification and a united country. Facing the strategic ambiguity of the US, and Taiwan's desire for status quo, China doubles down on its total conviction that it is right and that its proposal is the only viable one. Like many fired by a single cause, China's steadfastness of purpose is the source of its strength, but it is simultaneously the cause of its weakness. Its message's remorseless focus on the ultimate objective makes it a hard one with which to win hearts and minds on the island. That accounts for the negative reception given to it and for the rise of antipathetic voices captured in the polling figures cited earlier on.

There is another problem too. While it is easy to say that the aim is reunification, there are many paths that could be taken to get there, and the destination could take many forms. The 'One Country, Two Systems' rubric offered the framework China believed was best. The retrocession of Hong Kong in 1997 even offered some idea of how it might look like in reality, because that was undertaken on the same basis. In the years before the return of Hong Kong to China, Taiwanese might theoretically at least have found some upside in the idea; but once it existed in reality, the prospect of reunification became increasingly unattractive. The tightening restrictions on Hong Kong's political and cultural life, particularly since 2010, have had a big impact on cross-strait relations, with people in Taiwan watching freedoms they once assumed to be untouchable in Hong Kong slowly dissolve.

Despite the protests in the city in 2019, the Beijing government passed a powerful new law for Hong Kong a year later, in a direct intervention by central government in local affairs.

The title of the legislation, 'Safeguarding National Security in the Hong Kong Special Administrative Region', left little to the imagination; clauses made it an offence to criticize the PRC's leadership, or to commit acts – written or otherwise – that could be construed as promoting separatism. As with many laws in China, its terms were deliberately broad and subject to interpretation. Courts have therefore tended to apply the strictest reading of them, rather than attract the wrath of their political masters. This was vividly illustrated by the treatment of figures such as the former owner of the *Apple Daily* newspaper, Jimmy Lai. He was initially sentenced to thirteen months in prison in December 2021, and then received a further term of more than five years for alleged fraud in 2022, before being put on trial in December 2023 accused of colluding with foreign forces (an offence that carries a life sentence). Such high-profile events have increased distrust in the once highly regarded rule of law in Hong Kong, and made Taiwanese profoundly sceptical that any deal offered by China could be friendly and lasting. The bottom line is that once sovereignty is decided in Beijing's favour, Taiwan, like Hong Kong today, will be subject to its vagaries and at its mercy. Better to be free and go it alone, unrecognized by its vast neighbour, than be reunited with it and decidedly unfree.

Taiwan's China Policy

For these and other reasons, to China's 'yes, yes, yes' on unification, it seems Taiwan has worked itself into a position of forever saying 'no, no, no'. Nowhere needs a China policy quite as much or as urgently as Taiwan. And no one wrestles with the quandary of how to balance security needs on the one hand, and economic ones on the other, quite as intensely. In 2022 alone, China and Hong Kong accounted for 42 per cent of the island's exports (America came in at only 15 per cent).[13] Between 1991 and the end of 2022, according to Taiwanese government figures, 45,195 instances of investment in China had been approved, totalling US$203.33 billion.[14] This degree of interconnectivity and economic exposure means finding boundaries has proved extremely challenging, but also utterly necessary.

Up to the late 1980s, Taiwan's position on China was very straightforward. It did not recognize the legitimacy of the Beijing government, and did not allow trade and investment, or any direct links, with the mainland, whether businesses, government officials or even private citizens. It lifted restrictions on its citizens travelling across the strait only in 1987. The results of this opening up were frequently mixed. All too often, Taiwanese visitors found themselves subject to demands for luxury goods or financial support, with their families still on the mainland regarding them as prospective wealthy sponsors of their less well-off relatives. They were often shocked by the lack of development and by the widespread poverty that still prevailed, particularly in rural China. Repeatedly, the result of these visits for both sides was disillusionment and alienation.

A similar process of moving from idealism to a harsher, more realistic view occurred when investment in and business with China were allowed from the early 1990s. Taiwanese who went to exploit the new manufacturing opportunities now open to them across the mainland often found the general business environment extremely tough. Despite a common language and the assumption of some level of cultural connection, there were many bitter lessons, as business people reported being embezzled, cheated and sometimes had their intellectual property stolen by Chinese partners. Perhaps behind all of these issues there was a simple lack of alignment in terms of expectations and objectives. Both sides initially often assumed they were more similar to each other than they actually were, and only further on in their relationship discovered major differences in what they wanted, and how they wished to go about things.

The evolution of a Taiwanese cross-strait policy from total lack of contact to more direct links and mutual involvement has proved torturous. During the Lee Teng-hui era, informal discussions in Hong Kong in 1992 between China and Taiwan resulted in a form of words that created a framework for building relations while recognizing the considerable differences between the two parties. Both accepted that there was 'one China', but did not specifically state what that China was. This mirrored the ambiguity of the One China policies employed by other countries to steer their way through the minefield of cross-strait relations. The framework was akin to two people agreeing to use the same word, but giving it completely different meanings.

This position came to be called the '1992 Consensus'. While it has never formed an official part of Taiwanese policy, it did create a new atmosphere of dialogue and discussion on both sides. The Chinese established the Association for Relations across the Straits in 1991, which supported academic collaboration, and exchanges between ordinary people through travel, tourism and participation in sports and other tournaments; the Taiwanese reciprocated with the Straits Affairs Foundation. Ostensibly intended to address mainly technical issues – such as possible common standards for the trade of goods, or the potential mutual recognition of educational qualifications – they did allow some form of direct contact and space for shared debate. Scholars and think-tankers were able to engage in semi-official discussions. At the very least, the two sides were able to hear what each other was saying.

As the Lee Teng-hui presidency went on, it increasingly issued statements that asserted greater autonomy for Taiwan and supported the development of a stronger Taiwanese consciousness. The Taiwanese presidential election campaign of 1995–6 – which had elicited such a robust response from Beijing, in the form of military exercises in the strait – culminated in an outcome that China was deeply unhappy with: the landslide success of Lee. This showed for the first time the real challenges of dealing with Taiwan as a democracy, rather than the autocracy it had once been. Public opinion now had to be factored in. Lee himself mapped out a clear enough policy approach to the island's large neighbour. Reunification was accepted as an endpoint, but only if both sides fully committed to accomplishing it peacefully, and only once China itself had become a democracy. Lee wrote that 'the "one country, two systems" formula will not help bring democracy to the whole of China . . . A reunified China that is closed and autocratic would necessarily provoke anxiety in the neighbouring countries.' His proposal was that only with 'the implementation of a comprehensive democratic system, through the rule of law and transparent political processes will trust be enhanced'. This scenario presented only one viable route to reunification.[15]

As mentioned in Chapter 3, Lee himself went on to articulate a far more contentious approach, towards the end of his time in office. In an interview in July 1999 with the German radio station Deutsche Welle, he said that relations across the strait were on a 'special state-to-state' basis.[16] This attempt to upgrade the accepted status of Taiwan caused immediate reaction in Beijing, which predictably condemned his words. The US also expressed dismay, because while it did not support Beijing's stance of seeking unification on its own terms, nor did it stand by Taiwan going for unilateral independence. The approach was quietly dropped, though Lee's successor, Chen Shui-bian, at times skirted close to declaring that China and Taiwan were equals and needed to relate to each other as separate sovereign states. In the end, American pressure and the lack of strong domestic support, with most people wanting to maintain the status quo, prevented him going further.

Speaking in 2006, Chen outlined four key aims in cross-strait relations: sovereignty, democracy, peace and parity. 'The ultimate decision on Taiwan's future,' he stated, 'must and will be made by the 23 million people of Taiwan of their own free will.'[17] Attempts to promote his strategy of greater 'Taiwanization', however, antagonized and angered Beijing. The Chinese Foreign Minister in 2007, Li Zhaoxing, declared that Chen was merely a 'local' leader: 'Don't listen to local leaders,' he warned. 'Whoever wants to split away will become a criminal in history.'[18]

Chen's successor, Ma Ying-jeou, maintained a 'three noes' position during his presidential campaign in 2007, referring to policies adopted in the 1970s but updated for the new, more mutually involved situation with the mainland. Under his presidency, he promised, there would be 'no unification, no independence and no use of force'.[19] In power, Ma tried to square the circle by supporting closer links with China without these becoming cloying or dangerous. Most were economic in nature: trade was encouraged, Chinese investment allowed into the island, and greater daily links were nurtured between ordinary people on either side of the strait. Initially, Ma's miracle appeared to work. His efforts were seen as beneficial, with the severe economic recession in 2009 superseded by growth and greater prosperity a year later. For this, Ma was re-elected in 2012. But his attempts, during his second term, to extend the existing trade agreements with China into the far more sensitive and extensive financial and services sectors led to protests, the storming of the Legislative Assembly, and a retreat by Ma's government. The trade deal was put on hold. It has yet to be revived, and is unlikely ever to become adopted in its current form.

Under Tsai Ing-wen, the approach has been to stress the non-negotiability of Taiwan's political values. Based on the principles of 'peace, parity, democracy and dialogue', she refused to recognize the 1992 Consensus in the years before her presidency, which was interpreted by Beijing as a sign that she had doubts about the idea of one China itself. All indications are that William Lai Ching-te, her successor, will hold to this line too. As a somewhat inauspicious sign of how the current frostiness and hostility between both sides is likely to continue, a few days after Lai's election in January 2024, the tiny island nation of Nauru – one of the final countries still to recognize Taiwan – shifted its diplomatic allegiance to Beijing. This brings the total down to eleven, plus the Holy See, and shows that China is actively continuing its campaign to ensure Taiwan remains isolated.

Lines of Least Resistance: China's Dual-track Approach

The details of China's Taiwan policy have not remained static, despite Beijing's insistence on key non-negotiable overarching objectives. In 2000, the then premier, Zhu Rongji, stated fiercely that a vote for the DPP candidate, Chen Shui-bian, in that year's presidential election was akin to a vote for conflict and war. As in the 1996 election, attempts by the Chinese government to directly influence public opinion in Taiwan backfired, with Chen successfully voted in despite these stern warnings, just as Lee was four years earlier. Learning from this, China has tended to remain silent in subsequent elections. Despite this, there have been claims it has conducted wide-scale misinformation campaigns online, and attempted to achieve the same sort of election interference that Russia stood accused of in the US 2016 presidential campaign.[20]

Nevertheless, China now faces pushback from America, and evidence in Taiwan that fewer and fewer people find its proposals attractive, as highlighted by the surveys mentioned earlier. One has to ask, then, why has the Chinese government persisted with a strategy that increasingly seems to have failed? And why, in light of this, has its stance not become more pragmatic and flexible, but in many ways the opposite?

Since 1990, as China has been growing more powerful, its relations with Taiwan have broadly followed two tracks. Taiwanese have called these the 'carrot and stick'. Economic, material bonds have flourished, creating a new depth of interconnectedness. But since 2012, Xi nationalist populism has raised the profile of the Taiwan question, and hinted increasingly strongly that a resolution must now occur. Speaking to a visiting delegation from Taiwan in 2014, Xi made this patently clear when he said the current unsolved problem could not be handed down from generation to generation. He said the same thing four years later, when he met the former Taiwanese politician Lien Chan. These statements show that, for the leadership in Beijing, the clock is ticking on Taiwan's status.[21]

Xi Jinping knows something of Taiwan; he is engaging with a matter where he is not entirely lacking in past experience and history. His wife, the famous singer Peng Liyuan, had an uncle on the island (Li Hsin-kai who died in 2016), and indeed visited Taiwan as part of a cultural group in 1997.[22] Xi's own connection goes back to his sixteen years as an official in the southeastern province of Fujian. One of the great economic dynamos of the country, this was the place where Xi cut his political teeth, and started developing the practice of power that led to his final elevation as head of the Communist Party almost three decades later.

Xi arrived in Xiamen city to take up his first post in the province in 1985. It was here that he married Peng, his second wife, after the breakdown of his brief first marriage (that relationship had ended because his spouse had wanted to go abroad, but he insisted on staying in China). His path to becoming an official had been a rocky one. Xi was the child of senior leaders from the Maoist era. His father, Xi Zhongxun, had been a key figure in charge of culture when he was placed under house arrest in the early 1960s for allowing the publication of a novel accused of offering oblique criticism of the supreme leader, Mao Zedong. To be blamed for something of that nature was a career death sentence; indeed, Xi senior was lucky to escape with a lengthy detention rather than actual execution, an all too common fate for others who fell from favour at this time. Not only did he survive, but almost two decades later he was fully rehabilitated, playing a key role in the Deng Xiaoping era reforms as a leader in Guangdong, southern China, one of the key sites for the economic and investment changes sweeping the country.

His father's travails affected Xi. He went from being a member of the elite, with all the perks and privileges in terms of housing and education, to a more precarious existence. In his early teens, he had to look after himself, with his mother absent for long stretches because of her own official job in a government think tank. Things grew worse when the Cultural Revolution hit. Xi's family background was the least advantageous kind to have then. It typified the sense of entitlement and what some commentators called the loyal 'Red Communist' aristocracy, which Mao's most radical supporters despised. Aged only sixteen, he was sent out of Beijing to one of the most impoverished areas in central China. In the region of Yan'an, in Shaanxi province, he made his home for the next seven years. Around 1973, he took a chance and submitted ten applications to join the Communist Party. The organization he was to end up leading rejected him nine times because of his family background, before finally allowing him entry.

Xi became a civilian politician via a short stint in the military leadership. For reasons which remain unclear to this day, he left the relative comfort and stability of the latter for a short spell as a village leader, and then the years in Fujian. They are important for the Taiwan story because it was here, in the early 1990s, that he had a front-row seat on the new relationship with the island. Taiwanese were starting to come to the province as never before. China's central government wanted their technology, investment and know-how. Of all the allies in the growth mission for the country, Taiwanese with their advanced economy and their manufacturing ability were amongst the most promising.[23]

Xi remained in Fujian, rising up the ranks of the provincial leadership, throughout the few years of the first Taiwanese wave of trade and cooperation. Taiwanese business people (the Taishang) were familiar figures, tens of thousands of them making the province their place of work, and many living there most of the year. In the 1995–6 crisis, as the central government was trying to intimidate the Taiwanese electorate by all too realistic military drills in the waters around their island, Xi would have been a first-hand witness both to the Chinese actions and to the American response – the sending of two aircraft carriers to the region.

What was distinctive about Xi's outlook even back then, from interviews he undertook at the time and pieces that he wrote, was a clear notion of the division between politics and business. The great flow of Taiwanese capital and enterprises into the mainland created sources of wealth that everyone, not just the new entrepreneurs in China, wanted a piece of. Officials were not immune. In 1998, a massive scandal erupted. A Fujian businessman, Lai Changxing, through his Yuanhua Group, was involved in a US$10 billion smuggling network. When it came to light, the dreaded anti-corruption enforcers from Beijing found links deep within the local government, extending right to the top. Officials were removed from power, many handed steep prison sentences. Lai himself managed to flee, reaching Canada and living in exile there till 2011, when he was extradited back to China. He is currently serving a life sentence for his crimes.

Xi was not one of the officials brought down or even touched by the scandal. In this respect, he was in a minority. But the event clearly left its mark on him. The Party had many enemies, but perhaps the most deadly was itself. Corruption was eating away at its soul. It was hard to distinguish public servants from business people. Everyone was on the make, with immense sums disappearing from the state's coffers as individuals used their official positions to siphon off their ill-gotten gains to their cronies and personal networks. The Party took an ad hoc approach, sometimes clamping down to frighten people into temporary obedience and good behaviour. But, as scholar Andrew Wedeman pointed out, statistically it was a relatively safe bet that if you were corrupt, you were unlikely to be caught. One very good reason was that you were invariably surrounded by people just as complicit and guilty as you.[24]

The lessons of Fujian stayed with Xi when he climbed further up the Communist Party's greasy pole. Rewarded for his decade and a half of service on the front line between China and Taiwan, he was assigned to the wealthy central coastal province of Zhejiang, adjacent to Shanghai, in 2002. There the lectures and homilies from him continued unabated on the importance of the Party constantly fighting corruption and ensuring it was clean and purely devoted to politics. 'People,' Xi said in 2005, 'need to look not just at how cadres speak, but what they do.' And just as a fish rots from the head so, in the Party, the moral fibre of the top leadership was key. Misbehaviour, if it occurred there, would spread its malign influence throughout the whole of the body.[25]

Once Xi came to power as leader of the Communist Party and national president after the long years in the provinces, his political programme became clear quite quickly. The Party needed to clean up its act. On his first day as premier, on 15 November 2012, he made that abundantly plain. Speaking like a stern bishop admonishing a flock that had strayed, he warned: 'The whole party must be vigilant. The metal itself must be hard to be turned into iron. Our responsibility is to work with all comrades in the party to be resolute in ensuring that the party supervises its own conduct; enforces strict discipline.' Above all, it had to 'maintain close ties with the people'.[26] An anti-corruption campaign ensued, felling 'tigers and flies', the high and the low. Former top leaders were caught in the traps that were laid, overturning convention. Zhou Yongkang was someone who had sat beside Xi at the cabinet table of the Politburo – the supreme decision-making body running the country – for five years. Even so, he was prosecuted for corruption, expelled from the Party and given a life sentence. Thousands lower down the hierarchy were also swept away.

The outside world may have interpreted this as a power grab. But Xi himself rebuffed the accusation. Speaking while visiting the US in 2016, he said that this was no 'House of Cards' scenario (a reference to the popular political thriller being screened at the time).[27] It was about creating at least some degree of domestic support in China for a party that had come to be regarded during the years of the country's rapid growth and enrichment as an impediment rather than an asset. Its officials were viewed with suspicion and disdain by the public, seen largely as figures who were always looking for their own cut. If this continued, Xi made clear, at some point it would shatter the social contract, creating a vast backlash of the sort that had ejected the Nationalists from power over the whole of China seven decades before and put the Communists in their place.

Xi is a populist, pursuing the same 'drain the swamp' narrative that Donald Trump did in America during his 2016 election campaign. He wants to make China great again. That means bringing back Taiwan. The island has always mattered to Chinese leaders, but today it matters more than ever. The problem for the rest of the world is that, in recent years in China, public confidence in the government – at least in this part of its foreign policy – and the country's increased military capacity have aligned. To add to the mix, the Chinese authorities are living in a world where, since 2010, regard for the West economically and politically amongst many Chinese has eroded. The election of Trump; the confusion and travails in the European Union with events such as Brexit; the invasion of Ukraine by Russia; and finally the explosion of war in the Middle East and the impact of that on the wider world – all of these have reinforced in the minds of leaders like Xi that they might have their own problems, but the rest of the world is chaotic, unpredictable and declining in power. 'China the Winner' is Xi's theme. And for Taiwan that means offering the island a simple choice: join the winning team today on your terms; or later, on ours. But join you will have to.

Xi Jinping's Taiwan Dream

A rational politician on the mainland looking at the surveys of Taiwanese views of China, and at the outcome of elections on the island since 2016, would probably conclude that something had gone badly wrong in their approach. Almost every step of the way in the last decade, China has used words and promoted actions and policies that have served to alienate the population of what it says is part of its country. Rather than using Hong Kong as a reassuring model of how 'One Country, Two Systems' might work, it has made it the precise opposite. Instead of building on the platform offered for its soft power and cultural influence during the Ma Ying-jeou years, China has responded to his successor, Tsai Ing-wen, with shrillness and intolerance. Taiwanese have been detained when visiting the mainland, with one, Yang Chih-yuan, missing since late 2022.[28] In an event on the island nation of Fiji in 2020, Chinese diplomats reportedly arrived at an official reception which Taiwanese counterparts were present at and started a fight. One of the Taiwanese ended up in hospital.[29] A few years earlier in 2014, at an academic conference in Braga, Portugal, Chinese officials from the Han Ban educational organization in Beijing, which supports Confucius Institutes globally, took booklets with references to the Taiwanese Chiang Ching-kuo Foundation and tore the offending pages out. They apparently fled the country before local authorities could question them.[30]

Events like these – and there are many more that could be cited – mean it is hardly surprising that views in Taiwan have hardened towards China. This is not just about what happens in public, but also how things are in any formal contact between representatives from either side. One senior official in the Taiwanese government who has had to deal with Chinese interlocutors told me in 2017 how their opposite numbers 'did not act and speak reasonably' and were 'arrogant and abrasive'.

China is usually a rational actor. But when it comes to Taiwan, the heart takes charge over the head. The island as a spiritual and symbolic issue matters hugely. Xi is not the first leader to talk about the need for a resolution. Jiang Zemin used equally pressing words in the late 1990s. But Xi is the first to lead a China that is economically and militarily in a position to do something about achieving its aims. And he has long supported a form of Chinese nationalism where reunification takes a prominent role. 'National rejuvenation' is a key phrase in his politics. In 2014, he and his ideologues – the most prominent of whom, Wang Huning, was subsequently given the role of coordinating Beijing's Taiwan policy, in 2023 – crafted the 'China Dream' slogan. A major component of this was the idea of a country that had lain the ghosts from its past to rest. Patriotic education campaigns in Chinese schools from the 1990s have embedded the sense of people living in a country carved up, humiliated and victimized by colonizers and outsiders for much of its modern history. The period from the Anglo-Chinese Wars of 1839–60 to the Sino-Japanese War of 1937–45 is described as 'the century of humiliation'. Xi's promise to the Chinese people is that continuous, stable, strong rule by the Communist Party is the best bet to ensure that this misery is never repeated. The retrocession of Hong Kong in 1997 and Macau in 1999 after long possession by foreigners was part of the process of bringing the great unified Chinese state back together. The return of Taiwan is the culmination of this.

Nationalism in Xi's China works increasingly like a state religion. It is a church bolstered by the work of his colleague Wang Huning, who is the architect of this new style of domestic politics, where the onus is on pride and confidence based on Chinese identity and culture. The great emerging middle class, living in cities, working in the services sector, owning their homes, may feel little interest in 'Socialism with Chinese Characteristics and Xi Jinping Thought for the New Era' – the clunky title of the current key Party ideology. But they do respond to the idea that their country is a great and powerful one, a place that is now wealthier and better off than at any other time in modern history, and which has a glorious cultural heritage. Like the patriotic everywhere, they like to see their country succeed.

This patriotism is fertile territory for a politician. It is no wonder that Xi tills its soil relentlessly. 'China is a great country with a great civilization,' he declared in his New Year address for 2024. 'Across this vast expanse of land, wisps of smoke in deserts of the north and drizzles in the south invoke our fond memory of many millennium-old stories,' he went on, listing some of them. 'All this stands as testament to the time-honoured history of China and its splendid civilization. And all this is the source from which our confidence and strength are derived.'[31] These are not just rhetorical flourishes: Xi means what he says. More than anything else, this is the heart of his exhortation of Chinese people to continue supporting the government he leads. Those that underestimate the force of this in domestic Chinese politics do so at their peril.

Taiwan is also important for Xi and his fellow leaders because of its symbolism. The great Chinese state that currently exists is a confection, its various additions and expansions over the centuries making it what it is today. Its borders have been characterized by constant movement. Taiwan's tale is not a straightforward part of this wider story, as we have seen. Its inclusion, with the Qing conquest of the island in 1683, was more by accident than design.

Despite this complex, often scrappy past, these ancient ideas of unity, harmony and a Chinese world unified under heaven swirl around in the almost patriarchal attitude Beijing has towards Taiwan. Its separate existence is a continuing wound in Chinese nationalism under Xi. It is a reminder of how China remains an incomplete polity, with part of its ability to dictate its own affairs still in the hands of others. Chinese leaders attribute the new currents of independence and separateness on the island to the interference and manipulation of outsiders. America comes into the frame here. In China's eyes, Washington's support of Taipei over the decades – economically and militarily – has resulted in the situation today. Taiwan therefore figures as a symbol of continuing foreign interference in China, of the violation of its integrity, and of attempts to continue to control and coerce it.

Finally, Taiwan matters to Xi Jinping for strategic reasons. Imagine the situation. Off the coast of the US, a small island operates by a totally different political system. It is the recipient of massive aid and support from a far larger, more distant power, which shares its values. How would the US respond in this sort of scenario, and to what lengths would it go? We know the answer to this. In the early 1960s, Communist Cuba under Fidel Castro attempted to deepen its links with the Soviet Union by hosting nuclear warheads. The US reacted by blockading the island and demanding the missiles be withdrawn. Eventually, the USSR backed down. But the crisis is widely regarded as the one moment since the end of the Second World War when the globe came nearest to nuclear Armageddon. Cuba and Taiwan have many differences – not least concerning their status as nations and the fact that the US is not claiming sovereignty over its neighbour in the way China is. And yet it is instructive how much unease powers as dissimilar as America and China feel when faced by islands with contrasting political systems sitting just off their coasts.

The US has never attempted to help Taiwan nuclearize in the way the USSR did in the early 1960s with Cuba. But it has been a major supplier of weaponry and military technology to the island. That continues today. There are sound arguments for why it has done this, but that doesn't make the Chinese response irrational, even if its manner might strike critics as unpalatable. Taiwan occupies the centre of space that is of massive strategic importance to the People's Republic. It means that an ally and client of the US sits at the heart of key supply routes for the Chinese economy, and critical security interests. The saga of the maritime claims in the South and East China Seas, which China has pursued since the 1990s with increasing assertiveness, is not just a matter of resources and issues of historic sovereignty. It is about China securing a protective zone around itself, which it controls, in order to keep potential enemies at bay.

What Will Xi Do?

The Xi epoch has proved a heady one. Its character can be heard, loud and clear, in the popular slogans issued by the

Chinese government since 2013: 'a common destiny for the new era', 'national rejuvenation', the 'China Dream'. That Xi himself managed to remove restrictions on how long he can stay in power, gaining a third term as the Party's boss in 2022, arouses the suspicion that this is a man with ambitious plans and impressive visions who wants to leave behind him a lasting legacy.

Previous leaders talked of the historic mission to retake Taiwan and fulfil the dream of a reunified Chinese nation. But none were in the position to do much about it. They talked of centuries or decades. But as in so many other spheres, from the economic to the social, change in China is accelerating. The future arrives quicker and quicker these days. Increasingly, the question being asked by the rest of the world is not whether Xi plans to invade Taiwan, but when.

While there seems to be agreement that China does intend some kind of move towards unification, there is less consensus when it comes to time frames. Speaking in October 2021, Taiwanese Minister of Defence Chiu Kuo-cheng stated that China intended to make a move as soon as 2025.[32] Twelve months later, his US counterpart, Secretary of Defense Lloyd Austin, was more sanguine. 'I don't see an imminent invasion,' he told CNN. 'What we do see is China moving to establish what we would call a new normal.'[33] In November 2023, Song Tao, a senior official dealing with Taiwanese affairs in China, said that there were 'two paths of peace and war, prosperity or decline', for cross-strait relations.[34] Even Xi Jinping has waded in, with reports that he has told his military to be ready by 2027 to launch an attack.[35] Tsai Ing-wen, however, has kept calm. 'My thought is perhaps this is not a time for them to consider a major invasion of Taiwan,' she informed a US interviewer in late 2023, 'largely because of the economic, financial and political challenges, but also because the international community has made it loud and clear that war is not an option and that peace and stability serves everyone's interest.'[36]

In view of all this speculation, the best we can do is to admit that nobody – not even Xi himself – knows what will happen. All we can acknowledge is that the Taiwan issue matters at the deepest level to China, and that assumptions that it cannot or will not do anything are unfeasible. What an attack might entail will be discussed in Chapter 7. But the mindset of Beijing is currently set on a course where Taiwan joining the mainland is inevitable, not hypothetical.

Here is the situation today. Everything about what will happen with Taiwan rests in the hands of one man, a politician in his seventies in Beijing, who has never visited the island, and in recent years has had very limited contact with its leaders. Even a second meeting with the figure he knows best in Taiwan's politics, Ma Ying-jeou, in Beijing in 2024, is unlikely to have exposed him to representative public opinion on the island, given Ma's current unpopularity and marginal status. Xi's era may seem perpetual today, but at some point it will come to an end. Unification would clearly be the achievement that writes him into the history books as a great Chinese leader. This is a tantalizing prospect; it may prove irresistible. At some point in the near future, his advisors will present him with the options. They may even want to gloss over the challenges, and please him with best-case scenarios. At that moment, he will need to decide whether to act, or to stick with the status quo. Personal issues, such as the need for a legacy, or domestic political ones – such as the state of the Chinese economy and the need for something that will garner public support – might weigh on his mind. Then there will be the stance of the US, which will be decisive. Suspicions that it might not counter any move will increase the confidence of the hawks in China and their proposals to finally act.

If Xi does decide to do something, we will immediately enter a new world. It will be a terrifying and chaotic one. It will see the US and China pitted against each other in ways they have managed to avoid since the Korean War more than seventy years ago. Everyone on the planet will be affected. Xi will no doubt be aware of this, as he sits, contemplating what he will need to instruct his military to do. The most worrying thought is that he may believe he has no options. Red lines may have been crossed. The irresistible logic of Chinese nationalism and the march to greatness don't offer easy exit ramps. As with the build-up to the First World War, the globe would have sleepwalked into conflict. But this time it could be terminal. That is why the China–Taiwan issue needs the commitment and attention of the rest of the world.

6.   *Taiwan and the US: Allies Indeed?*

On the morning of 2 August 2022, one of the most intensely studied things on the internet was the movements of a single aircraft. Millions of people online were watching as the image of the plane edged from its previous stopping point, Kuala Lumpur in Malaysia, northeast across the South China Sea towards the island of Taiwan. A little before eleven in the morning, it finally landed at Taoyuan international airport near Taipei. Its arrival on the island prompted an immediate response from Beijing, with Foreign Minister Wang Yi labelling the plane's landing 'manic, irresponsible and irrational'.[1] Public figures back in the US condemned what was happening as well. Thomas Friedman, the American author and journalist, said the visit was 'utterly reckless'.[2] Others regarded it as ill thought-out and provocative. Even the Biden administration itself was lukewarm, making clear the flight had no official approval.[3]

All of this excitement was due to the fact that the chief passenger travelling to Taipei that day was Nancy Pelosi, the 82-year-old Speaker of the House of Representatives and the third highest-ranking US official after the president and vice president. Pelosi was expected to lose her position at the upcoming midterm elections a couple of months later (something that indeed came to pass). This was, therefore, a diplomatic swansong for a figure who had taken a characteristically strong position in support of Taiwan. In a newspaper article issued on the day of her arrival, Pelosi wrote that America 'must stand by

Taiwan, which is an island of resilience. Taiwan is a leader in governance . . . It is a leader in peace, security and economic dynamism: with an entrepreneurial spirit, culture of innovation and technological prowess that are envies of the world.'[4] She went on to describe the defence of the island as it stood against increased aggression and assertiveness from China as not just a regional issue. Why its predicament mattered so much for the US was simple: 'We cannot stand by as the [Chinese Communist Party] proceeds to threaten Taiwan – and democracy itself.' She was going to Taiwan to defend ideals and values. That was, in her view, why her visit was necessary.

The moment she stepped off the plane, there were consequences. The Chinese immediately started military exercises, encircling the island with jets for three days. There were follow-up 'drills' which disrupted shipping and civil aviation for a further few days. Chinese Dongfeng missiles were fired, along with nine other ballistic weapons launched from areas around the coast. Some landed in waters claimed as part of the economic territory of Japan, prompting Tokyo to lodge a protest. Incursions by the Chinese air force into the Taiwanese airspace had been increasing over the previous few years. Now they became the norm rather than the exception.

Pelosi's visit did have a precedent. In 1996, one of her predecessors as Speaker, the Republican Newt Gingrich, had also come to Taipei. But over the subsequent quarter of a century, things had changed dramatically. Taiwan had developed and deepened its democracy. China had become a far larger and more powerful economy. The US too had changed. By 2022, its domestic politics were highly partisan and divided, with distrust about China one of the few areas where Democrats and Republicans saw eye to eye. Trump's impact had been significant when president from 2017 to 2021. His approach to relations with China mainly focused on getting a better trade relationship that worked in America's favour rather than spending much time on human rights and democratic values. This had, on the one hand, simplified most issues to a calculation of where the US gained and where it lost in dealing with its main global contender. But on some other matters, tensions had escalated. Trade wars, arguments over military spending and rising bipartisan support for a stronger pushback against China's regional and international aims – such as its huge Belt and Road Initiative – were all now accepted ingredients of the new era. The mantra of cooperation and dialogue, which had been intoned since the 2000s, was replaced by hard-nosed realism. The Washington consensus now was that China was a threat that needed constant vigilance and pushback from the American giant.

Taiwan stood on the front line of this great struggle. In late 2016, as the world absorbed the shock of an imminent Trump presidency, the president-elect placed a call to his opposite number in Taipei, Tsai Ing-wen. As with the Pelosi visit, this was an unusual event. Since the first day of 1979, when America had shifted formal diplomatic recognition to the People's Republic in Beijing and opened up its embassy there three months later, direct contact at the most senior level with the government of Taiwan ceased completely. There were protocols in place that policed this strange situation. Specific officials, such as the Foreign Minister and the Defence Minister, were not allowed bilateral visits. Presidential contact of any sort was another red line.

Although Trump had not yet been inaugurated, his actions raised questions about what his approach to the Taiwan issue would be once he was ensconced in the Oval Office. Would he do as he had in other areas, and disregard convention? Would he even start to consider ignoring the most sensitive restrictions, such as having the Taiwanese president visit when he was in the White House? Any of these, at any time, would have been immediate triggers for Beijing. The fact that US–China relations were now more deeply competitive than ever before, and that China had more capacity to act if it so chose, only made matters more dangerous.

Unlike any other place, Taiwan has to pay close attention to relations between the two most powerful nations on the planet. A 'shrimp caught between two whales', as a popular Taiwanese saying puts it, the island has to carefully tend how it works with Washington, and how it manages the tensions with Beijing. The attention of Donald Trump turned out to be a classic mixed blessing. The Taiwanese, as the Foreign Minister at the time, Joseph Wu, stated, wanted the outside world to understand their situation, and to pay attention to what was happening in their region. Solidarity from other countries was important.[5] But that didn't mean Taiwan wanted the kind of attention that would cause Beijing to escalate its response and start taking actions potentially leading to all-out war. People on the island understood well how their status touched on deep-seated sensitivities and aroused visceral feelings from China. The last thing Taipei wanted was to become a plaything in the great global game between the two superpowers – a situation where it truly would be unable to control its own future.

Taiwan's US Friendship: The Early Days

Looking at events after the Second World War shows us that the deepening involvement of the US in Taiwanese affairs was not inevitable. The immediate post-war president, Harry Truman, and his administration had grown disillusioned with the Nationalists and increasingly contemptuous of the leadership of Chiang Kai-shek. The aid they had given in the Civil War to fight the Communists had ended up proving to be a failed investment. Much of it seemed to have been frittered away in corruption and poor management. What mattered, however, was not so much Taiwan as an issue per se, but global geopolitics. The victory of Mao's Communist forces was seen as that of a staunch ally of the USSR. The world was falling to the forces of the totalitarian left.

For the US, when the Korean War started in 1950, the aim was very simple – to defend liberal democracy. There was a new great cause: to create a world of shared values against the threat of an alternative that was authoritarian, collectivist and anti-capitalist. Defence of Taiwan figured in that strategy, and it gave the threatened regime of Chiang Kai-shek a new lease of life. America showed this renewed commitment in December 1954, when it signed the mutual defence pact that came into effect the following year. It also continued to confer diplomatic recognition on the island. Significantly, at the same time it cut almost all ties with the new regime in Beijing, imposing sanctions and embargoes that even the British, with their continuing interests in Hong Kong and their official representation in Beijing, had to abide by.

For more than a decade after this, the US supplied Taiwan with generous aid along with military and other forms of technical assistance. Taiwan became a link in the chain of treaty alliances that stretched across the Asia Pacific region, an informal part of the US-led world. Japan, South Korea and the Philippines all hosted American troops and had defence pacts with Washington. Taiwan sat in this network, able to procure advanced technology and even lobbying unsuccessfully for nuclear capability in the 1960s, when China acquired the nuclear bomb.

With the 1954 defence pact in place, the main tactical issue for America was the fear of being dragged into conflict by a Taiwanese administration assuming that Washington would need to come to its aid whatever it did with the mainland. Into the 1960s, as Chiang continued his autocratic rule, he never let up on the statement of his ultimate goal – reunification. Reconquest of the rest of China now under Communist rule remained the objective, with constant low-level clashes from the small islands that constituted Taiwan's territory close to the Fujian coast a first stepping stone to achieving this aim. American politicians frequently told Taiwan not to assume the US would take the island's side if things did escalate.

The ensnarement of the US by North Vietnamese Communist forces in the Vietnam War from the early 1960s eroded American public support for getting caught up in the wars of others halfway across the world. More than 58,000 US servicemen died in that conflict. Its ultimate unpopularity domestically played some role in the calculation of Richard Nixon when he became president in 1969 of creating a new set of alliances that would provide greater security for US interests. This was apposite in view of fears about the USSR's expansionist plans in Eastern Europe and Asia. Blocking these, and stopping what was called 'the domino effect' of Communism spreading further afield, into South and Southeast Asia, was key.

The origins of the US policy of strategic ambiguity on the issue of Taiwan's defence can be traced back to this era – to be supportive of Taiwan, but also ensure that the island did not exploit its relationship with the US to promote its claims against the mainland. The US's worst nightmare would have been a move by Chiang Kai-shek against the Communists, with his forces trying to launch a counter-invasion of the mainland. This would have obliged the US to intervene in order to reassert stability in an increasingly important region. Then it would be pitted against the most populous country in the world – one which, while still very poor, from the early 1960s had nuclear weapons, and possessed a formidable army, at least in terms of numbers. This was not desirable for the Americans.

The Great Betrayal

The early 1970s were a period of transition for the Taiwan issue for two reasons. The first was the arrival of the Nixon realists in the White House. In power from late 1968, they had engaged in a systemic rethink of America's foreign policy. The second was that a similar reappraisal was occurring at the same time, albeit in very different circumstances, in China. More pragmatic figures around the premier Zhou Enlai were pushing for an end to the years of isolation during the early period of the Cultural Revolution. This set in motion the rapprochement between the US and China only a few years later. The great tectonic fault lines that Taiwan sat on diplomatically were thus moving once again, with zero input from itself. In 1971, the changeover from Taiwan to the People's Republic representing China at the United Nations happened. Within a year, President Nixon was standing in Beijing. A Sino-American détente after two decades of iciness was underway.

Nixon was an unexpected figure to be in office when these dramatic changes happened. He had visited Taiwan in 1953, while vice president, and been a guest of Chiang Kai-shek.

Throughout this era, and into the 1960s, he was regarded as a strong opponent of Communism and a vocal critic of Beijing. But once within sight of power he became far more flexible as to which international partners he worked with. In the White House, along with his principal foreign policy advisor, Henry Kissinger, he implemented a realignment of America's global relationships. Both felt that the absence of the Chinese from the international multilateral system was increasingly anomalous, particularly as it was now abundantly clear that they did not belong to the same stable as the USSR, which figured in many ways as both countries' common enemy. In 1969, the true state of Russian and Chinese relations was revealed when the two nations clashed on China's northeast border in the region of the Ussuri River. Though the casualties on both sides were modest, it was obvious that these Communist neighbours were now deeply hostile to each other. For Kissinger and Nixon, opportunists to their fingertips and forever looking at the bigger picture, some sort of pact with Beijing now became possible. That pushed Taiwan into a wholly new position, because alliance with it became less of a priority in American strategic and diplomatic thinking.

All of this is evident from the ways in which Kissinger spoke on his famous secret visits to Beijing in late 1971, preparing for the presidential visit the following year. During his discussions with the Chinese premier Zhou Enlai about the conditions for this détente, Zhou stated that if the US was to normalize relations with Beijing, then it would need to 'withdraw all armed forces from the area of Taiwan . . . within a fixed period'. Kissinger did not disagree, responding that 'political evolution' – by which he meant the shift of diplomatic recognition from Taipei to Beijing – 'can start concurrently with our military withdrawal. It will take a somewhat longer period of time, but it can start at the same time.' Later in their conversation that day, Kissinger declared that 'we will not support the Taiwan Independence Movement . . . We will not support one China, one Taiwan.' The aim was to have 'recognition of the People's Republic of China as the sole legitimate government of China'. Talking further about the island's independence, Kissinger reiterated: 'We will give no support either direct or indirect.' If the Chinese had evidence of agitation for Taiwanese independence on the island, 'I will see that whatever is going on is stopped.' The Chinese needed to appreciate that Nixon was 'the only president who could conceivably do what I am discussing with you . . . Other political leaders might use more honeyed words, but would be destroyed by what is called the China [i.e. Taiwan] lobby in the U.S. if they ever tried to move even partially in the direction which I have described to you.'[6] Kissinger was making it unambiguously clear to his Chinese interlocutors that America was now willing to have a far closer relationship with the People's Republic, and to sacrifice its formal links with Taiwan in order to achieve this.

Some Taiwanese, when they learned of these discussions, regarded them as selling their country down the river. A somewhat careworn Chiang, approaching the end of his life in Taipei, met the news of Nixon's historic visit to China with a sense of fatalism. Whether a betrayal or not, it showed the new global order. During Nixon's encounter with an ailing Mao in Beijing, the ancient leader had uttered the throwaway remark that China 'can wait, maybe even a hundred years', for unification.[7] As the American president proceeded down to Shanghai towards the end of his visit, a communiqué set out Washington's new position. In this, the US recognized that there was only one China, and that Taiwan was part of China. The precise wording was all-important: 'The United States acknowledges that all Chinese on either side of the Taiwan Strait maintain there is but one China and that Taiwan is a part of China. The United States Government does not challenge that position. It reaffirms its interest in a peaceful settlement of the Taiwan question by the Chinese themselves.'[8]

That remains the official position to this day. 'Acknowledges', as explained earlier, meant no commitment to saying who, in the end, would be the sole legitimate government of the country. Maybe one day the Nationalists, or some other political force, would hold power in the People's Republic. The key thing was that, whatever happened, it had to be by agreement of all parties. If any aspect of that was lacking, then the status quo had to be preserved. No coercion from Taiwan or China could force the issue. The US was simply an honest bystander, not getting sucked into a domestic dispute, but remaining neutral.

Changing Sides

Only a few years later, in December 1978, the US's Deputy Secretary of State, Warren Christopher, had the unenviable task of going to Taipei to deliver some bad news in person. A crowd of 20,000 locals greeted his cavalcade as it wove its way towards the centre of Taipei. According to reports, 'Locked in the cars of their motorcade, the officials endured nearly an hour of thumping and pelting of their vehicles.'[9] Luckily no one was hurt. The anger was precipitated by suspicions of what precisely the bad news might be. A new joint communiqué issued by Beijing and Washington a fortnight earlier set out clearly what was about to happen. 'The United States of America and the People's Republic of China have agreed to recognize each other and to establish diplomatic relations as of January 1, 1979,' it stated.[10] While promising that cultural, commercial and other unofficial relations would be maintained with Taiwan, the communiqué noted that, as of 1 March 1979, the American ambassador and embassy would move to Beijing from Taipei.

Chiang Kai-shek had been dead four years by 1979. The response of his son Chiang Ching-kuo, who had inherited his mantle, was as fatalistic as the elder Chiang's had been over the loss of the UN seat at the start of the decade. Chiang junior showed in his actions during the 1980s that he believed Taiwan had to exist in a new framework, one it had been receiving stronger and stronger premonitions of. Had Nixon not been felled by the Watergate scandal in 1974, there was every likelihood that the US would have shifted its diplomatic recognition earlier. His removal slowed the process down, but it had an unstoppable momentum. Jimmy Carter, despite being a very different politician, was the incumbent in the White House when the decision was finally made.

The Taiwanese did have one source of comfort. Although the formal 1954 defence treaty with the Americans, with its strong reassurances and commitments to protect the security of the island, had ended, a new piece of legislation was now brought in. The Taiwan Relations Act of 1979 was not as solid as the treaty it replaced, but it did contain the provision that 'the President is directed to inform the Congress promptly of any threat to the security or the social or economic system of the people on Taiwan and any danger to the interests of the United States arising therefrom'. It then went on to specify that 'the President and the Congress shall determine . . . appropriate action by the United States in response to any such danger'. This was because of the US's commitment to 'the preservation and enhancement of the human rights of all the people on Taiwan'.[11] The reference to shared values was key. That was the basis on which the US and Taiwan would stand beside each other, despite all the changes that had recently happened.

But, to the surprise of many, it was Carter's successor, Ronald Reagan, who played the leading role in the final act of betrayal of the Taiwanese. Just like Nixon, his fellow Republican, Reagan had been a strong defender of Taiwan's autonomous status and its right to international political attention, before becoming president in 1981. He had even visited the island four times while governor of California. Such familiarity with Taiwan, and a long track record of opposing Communism, did not prevent him making a similar calculation to Nixon's a decade earlier. The USSR was the era's central problem. And China figured as a potential ally here. Maintaining positive relations with the PRC also mattered because of the unexpected economic reforms starting to have an impact there. American business saw a vast potential new market open up to them. Companies such as Coca-Cola and Ford had already started making inroads from 1980. Many more aimed to follow in their footsteps.

The 1982 US–China Communiqué focused on the critical issue of arms sales. These had been a perpetual sticking point during Kissinger's sparring with Zhou Enlai in 1971. America arming Taiwan was a massive problem for China – and the removal of US support in this area was crucial for Beijing. The 1982 communiqué stated that America 'does not seek to carry out a long-term policy of arms sales to Taiwan . . . [and] that it intends gradually to reduce its sale of arms to Taiwan, leading, over a period of time, to a final resolution'.[12] The island's greatest reassurance in the new, more uncertain situation had been the supply of US high-tech equipment to protect itself. The weakening of America's commitment to this created a world of even greater precariousness, forcing Taiwan to rethink the nature of its diplomacy.

To compound the problem, other countries following in the wake of the US were shifting their recognition to Beijing. The new China now emerging had a far more proactive foreign policy, with leaders such as Deng Xiaoping going to the US in 1979 and wooing the American public by wearing a ten-gallon hat at a Texan rodeo. Taiwan looked increasingly isolated and sidelined. For Taiwan's new leaders, such as Lee Teng-hui, the anointed successor of Chiang Ching-kuo who was already occupying senior positions in the early 1980s, the need to construct a more autonomous and distinctive path for the country in view of this seismic change was clear. The question was how to accomplish it.

The Years of Being Stranded

Throughout the 1980s and 1990s, Taiwan remained caught in the tides of US–China relations, and subject to their ebbs and flows. It existed like a boat being tossed around on waves whipped up by others. At first, while the US maintained a degree of idealism and hope for the situation in the People's Republic of China, Taiwan sank a little in its list of priorities. The 1980s were hard years for Taiwan as it adjusted to its new, more vulnerable and more complicated global role as an entity that was important, but not recognized.

The 1989 Tiananmen Square massacre of pro-democracy protestors in Beijing, and the international condemnation that followed, precipitated a much more fractious relationship between China and the US. America under President George

H. W. Bush did not break off contact with the senior Chinese leadership after the tragic events of 4 June that year, but it did rethink some of its previous assumptions. The dominant politician in China at the time, Deng Xiaoping, was clearly no closet reformer. The country under the Communist Party was not going to engage with the sort of liberalization seen in the USSR under Mikhail Gorbachev. The collapse of the Soviet Union only two years later, in 1991, reinforced Beijing in its conviction that it had to put all its resources into defending one-party rule or risk suffering the same demise as the older, and once far more powerful, Communist Party.

Taiwan was not passive in this situation. The greatest strategic choice it made – and one that subsequently proved to be a master stroke – was to embark on its own process of political reform. That aligned it more closely with the US's values, and created a deeper bond between the two countries. As a non-democracy, Taiwan was harder to defend as a close ally of the US. Washington could not continue to support a place that did not share its political ethos, even if it was sympathetic to Taiwan's right to self-determination. Becoming a democracy moved Taiwan into the 'free world' category, enabling it to earn the affinity and allegiance of many Americans who had previously not related greatly to the island's fate. The Taiwan Relations Act had given a key role to the House of Representatives with its requirement for US administrations to consult it on matters pertaining to Taiwan's defence. This meant that, for Taipei, lobbying the US Congress and maintaining good links with domestic politicians was now a sound investment.

Taiwan has proved astute over the years at spotting which American politicians might have brighter future prospects, and then cultivating them. One of the rising political stars that Taipei courted in the 1980s and early 1990s was Senator Bill

Clinton of Arkansas. He, like Reagan, was hosted in Taiwan during four visits, before his success in the 1992 presidential election. His promise to be harder on China and its human rights issues was one of the key planks of his campaign. While in office, he almost inevitably had to row back on some of his more hawkish language because of the importance of the business links being established by the likes of Boeing, which was starting to sell more and more planes into the emerging Chinese market, and General Motors, with its cars. But the ongoing democratization of Taiwan – with its first elections held under universal adult suffrage in 1991, and its historic 1996 presidential election – along with the expansion of other freedoms, such as a more independent media and judiciary, created shared ideological bonds.

In terms of official government policy, the US did not change its stance as defined in the various earlier communiqués. It continued to insist that there was one China, and that only mutual agreement and peaceful means could resolve the differences across the strait. But in reality even if there was one China, it existed in two parts that now operated by totally different systems. And, even more importantly, those differences were growing. As Taiwan was becoming a more established, multiparty democracy, China looked set to be the world's first Communist Party-dominated country to run a semi-capitalist economy.

The US responded to these unexpected developments by retreating from the Reaganite position of a decade earlier and restarting the supply of military equipment to Taiwan. The island still inserted itself as an issue in US–China relations, with politicians needing to demonstrate their position on protecting Taiwan's interests. It had become part of the narrative of the global onward march of democracy, a place like many others in the 1990s which had moved from autocracy towards a liberal political system, and which figured as a further demonstration that the future would be heading only in this direction. To defend Taiwan was to defend an ideal, not just a place.

Taiwan into the New Millennium

The instability that Taiwan–US relations were now prey to was typified by the presidency of George W. Bush. A few months into his term in office, in an interview with ABC News, he declared that America would 'do whatever it took to help Taiwan defend herself'.[13] Since the 1970s, the US had strenuously maintained its position of ambiguous neutrality, where uncertainty about how it might act if things deteriorated either side of the strait was regarded as a useful advantage. Bush's brief statement seemed to blow this out of the water by presenting Taiwan with a far more solid guarantee.

It was not a position that lasted long, however. Officials made clear that, despite the new president's words, the US's policy on Taiwan had not changed. It still regarded the issue as one that needed to be dealt with peacefully, by both sides. If either party launched a pre-emptive assault on the other, they could not assume what Washington's response would be. The terrorist attacks of 9/11, however, changed matters once again, and dramatically. China went from being a looming threat in Bush's eyes to a key ally in the War on Terror that he launched soon after. China's support for US action in Afghanistan, and its toleration of the military interventions that were to unfold in the Middle East, pushed Washington's commitment to Taiwan into the background.

A further new dimension was the role of increasingly volatile domestic politics in both the US and Taiwan. Democracy turned up unforeseen outcomes. Bush had not been expected to win against the Democrat challenger Al Gore in 2000. The success of the DPP's Chen Shui-bian was also one that many did not predict. For the US and China, this new, more independence-leaning Taiwanese figure posed significant challenges (even if they were very different ones depending on whether they were viewed from Washington or Beijing). Chen's provocative words on relations with China, and on Taiwan's status, worried many policymakers. His hints at Taiwan's right to full recognition as an autonomous, separate state required the US to constantly signal its disagreement. Bush himself developed a strong antipathy to Chen, with one Japanese report claiming that he was the president's 'least favourite democratically elected leader', and another carried by Taiwanese media going so far as to say that Bush had described him as 'a son of a bitch'.[14]

American collaboration with China in the 2000s was framed not just by the War against Terror but also by the fallout from the 2008 economic crisis. The security of Taiwan figured as a lower priority compared to the threats posed to America by these other objectives. At the same time, the more collaborative policy of Chen's successor, Ma Ying-jeou, with the mainland meant that the US could discreetly assign its relationship with Taiwan to the category of requiring some attention and cultivation, but not urgently. Taiwan and China seemed to be working things out between themselves, with little sign of any timetable either Beijing or Taipei might be working towards which might force things in ways not mutually agreed.

Three developments since 2012 have upturned that brief period of relative harmony. The first, as we saw in the last chapter, was the rise of Xi Jinping in China and the stronger and more vocal claims of historic rights over Taiwan he has made. These have only intensified in recent years as the mainland economy started to lag in 2023, and the challenges of keeping the great emerging middle class content increased. In this context, trumpeting that only the Communist Party could restore China's geographical integrity and retake Taiwan proved good domestic politics. Building public support through this uncompromising line has created a new basis for the Party's legitimacy.

The second development was in Taiwan, where the rule of the DPP since 2016 has returned the situation to its position in the early 2000s, with the government in Beijing facing the ruling party it most dislikes on the island. Direct contact between the political leaders of both places is now almost non-existent. The uncomfortable fact is that the world's potentially most lethal conflict currently has no one at the very top on either side keeping a close watch on the other's moods and intentions. Everything is mediated. And sometimes mediators can be the problem by promoting their own interests rather than those of the people they are shuttling between.

This brings us to the third development. America has all too often served as mediator-in-chief. It has maintained contact with China and Taiwan, with high-level meetings between Xi Jinping and President Biden at the end of 2023 – as well as more regular ministerial summits – and relatively frequent contact with Taiwan, albeit at a lower level. But the great issue now is that America is increasingly capricious and hard to predict, and its own politics are subject to dramatic changes. The election of Donald Trump in 2016 was an issue for Taiwan not so much for his character, but for his clearly insular view of the US, and his deep aversion towards entanglements in foreign affairs. Trump was supremely transactional. He constantly returned to the question of US forces' presence abroad and the cost of their deterrent effect, demanding that other countries needed to make bigger contributions to funding the North Atlantic Treaty Organization (NATO) and the deployment of American troops in Japan and South Korea.

Economically, too, President Trump was not a natural friend to Taiwan's interests. The Trans-Pacific Partnership (TPP) was a proposed free-trade agreement between twelve countries in the Asia Pacific region including Japan, Australia, Canada and Singapore. It was interpreted by commentators as an attempt to create a stronger trading and economic network that would counterbalance the increased dominance of China, which was not a proposed member. Even though Taiwan was not directly involved either, the agreement would have served the island's interests by potentially creating greater economic diversity across the region. But the TPP initiative was one of the early casualties of the Trump administration. On 30 January 2017, only a few days after the president's inauguration, the US formally withdrew from negotiations.

Trump proved hard to predict on his approach to Taiwan and to China generally. His early phone conversation in December 2016, while he was still president-elect, with President Tsai Ing-wen was the first direct contact at that level between the two countries since the US recognized the PRC in 1979. But he also referred to Xi Jinping as a 'brilliant' man, who 'ruled with an iron fist', praised him in 2018 for removing time limits on the role of the presidency, and flattered him to his face by calling him a 'king' during a state visit to Beijing in 2017.[15] This was all happening while senior administration officials around Trump were labelling China their country's greatest economic and security threat, and imposing tariffs and trade restrictions on its exports and investment.

Trump's Secretary of State, Mike Pompeo, was not entirely untypical. Guided by his advisor Maochun (Miles) Yu, he regarded the People's Republic as a bastion of anti-Christian evil, a place best described not as a mere competitor but as a diehard adversary that posed an existential threat to the values of the US-led free world. After Trump's defeat in 2020, on the administration's very last day in office, Pompeo adopted an even more overt position, declaring that the US should recognize Taiwanese independence.[16] Once out of office in 2022, he made a personal visit to Taiwan, during which he referred to the place as 'a great nation'.[17] Such language crossed a red line for Beijing. A spokesperson for the Ministry of Foreign Affairs pulled no punches when they labelled Pompeo 'a US politician whose credibility has been bankrupted . . . working for personal gains'. A commentator in the Chinese state-owned media added that 'his purpose was obvious as he wants to pour oil on the flames of the most sensitive issue of the Sino-US relations by spurring the US to go further in the direction of unilaterally changing the status quo of the Taiwan Straits'.[18]

Into this maelstrom, in the spring of 2023, dived the Right Honourable Elizabeth Truss MP. For forty-nine memorable days in September and October the previous year, she had served as Prime Minister of the United Kingdom, one of the US's closest allies. It was the shortest period in office of a British leader since the position of Prime Minister was established more than 250 years earlier. This has not prevented Truss from following Pompeo's lead and visiting Taiwan, where she demonstrated a similar lack of interest in the minutiae of the One China policy. For her, Taiwan was now the symbol of a great geopolitical struggle, somewhere 'on the frontline of the global battle for freedom', which needed an 'economic NATO' to protect it.[19]

Such visits represented the very mixed blessing that Taiwan's new prominence has brought with it. This was captured by criticism of Truss's visit expressed by a colleague in the Conservative Party, Alicia Kearns. Kearns (who was also chair of the influential parliamentary Foreign Affairs Committee) dismissed Truss's tour as 'Instagram diplomacy', continuing, 'Taiwanese people already have to live with more Chinese military manoeuvres because of Nancy Pelosi's visit. Liz Truss doesn't have any influence now – this is more about keeping herself relevant.'[20]

Taiwanese government officials are not naive. They know that out-of-office foreign dignitaries coming to declare support and solidarity with them are often driven as much by personal ambition as any particularly deep interest in the island's affairs per se. But, for the government in Taipei, the publicity and headlines these visits create ensure that the challenges they face each day are not forgotten by the outside world. This is crucial. Unable to have its president, Foreign Minister and Defence Minister travel as conventional top-level representatives to the vast majority of the world, Taiwan is often dependent on getting its message out when prominent people visit – even if the prominent people are hardly the ones it would most like to host. Unusually, Tsai Ing-wen herself was able to visit the US in April 2023, and had a meeting with Pelosi's successor as Speaker of the House, Kevin McCarthy.[21] Encounters like this were held in neutral locations, such as research foundations and universities, at arm's length from formal government. That helped preserve the fiction they were not official diplomatic state activity, but unofficial get-togethers – and therefore they carried no implications for America's position on the One China policy.

What Does Taiwan Want from the US?

In the last four decades, Taiwan has gone from famine to feast in its relations with the US. Now it seems that every American senator, congressman or aspiring presidential candidate wants to talk up the alliance with Taiwan and the US's sacrosanct mission to stand by it.

This surfeit of attention is both positive and negative for Taiwan. China and America, with their radically different political and social values, are involved in something far greater than a fight for military or economic dominance. They represent starkly contrasting world views, and conflicting ideas of global order. Their ways of operating are utterly different too. These are powers whose cultural outlooks are totally misaligned. America is a proselytizing believer in the universal validity of its values. China, with its far more transactional view of relationships, subscribes to the right to be localist and to opt out of the grand global rules that the US so vigorously promotes.

Taiwan – hybrid, diverse, pluralistic – sits between these two mighty poles. It maintains some elements of Chinese culture while embracing liberal multiparty democracy and civil society. Its potential as a tool for one pole to attack the other through makes it pivotal – and profoundly exposed. The last thing any country desiring greater sovereignty wants is to be the plaything of others, even if they are powerful allies.

Taiwan understands that, with the US, alliance is paramount – even if it is with a more unpredictable and unstable US. As Foreign Minister Joseph Wu said in December 2023, Taiwan needs weapons systems, military training and intelligence from its key partner. But it has to be reliant on its own resources as well, and practise self-defence. It also, he went on, needs the US to spell out to China the disastrous consequences for it if it were to attack Taiwan: the economic damage, the international condemnation, the multinational response. This shows that the island has powerful friends.[22] Such solidarity continues to be important.

The Taiwan–US–China nexus is the world's most consequential triangular relationship. Each party is linked to the others in important but distinct ways – the US and China as the world's economic and military superpowers; the US and Taiwan as allies based on shared ideas and values; Taiwan and China through their historic bonds and the emphasis Beijing currently places on them. The interdependence of these three players – so very different in size, outlook, culture and history – sits at the heart of geopolitics today.

Taiwan resides between China and America like a loved one trying to navigate between two ardent suitors. In the attempts by the two superpowers to win over the small island with their declarations of fidelity and care, Taiwan is all too aware that it is dealing with a couple of admirers who, if repelled, are likely to challenge their successful rival to a duel where the weapons won't be swords or pistols, but nuclear weapons. This is the single most dangerous scenario facing the world, one that could propel it crashing into a global conflict. Since the final decades of the twentieth century, ambiguity and commitment to the status quo have been the great peacemakers, allowing Taiwan, China and the US to coexist without major mishap. But the foundations on which this is based are vulnerable and could crumble very quickly.

No matter how much things might appear to have changed in the last few decades, we need to remind ourselves, every day, about why this policy was constructed, why it has worked so long, and why jettisoning or chipping away at it would cause a catastrophe. It might not be much of a defence as we head further into the twenty-first century. But, at the moment, it is the only one we have. To further undermine or even abandon it would be to court disaster.

7. What If a Cross-strait War Started?

This is a sign of how worrying things have become. On three occasions in 2021–2, when US President Joe Biden was asked if America would come to the aid of Taiwan if it were attacked by China, he unequivocally stated that it would. The implication was that the One China stance and strategic ambiguity were no longer US policy.

In an interview with ABC News in August 2021, Biden seemed to state that America had given the same security guarantee to Taiwan as it had to South Korea and Japan, its two key treaty allies in the Asia region. 'We made a sacred commitment . . . that if in fact anyone were to invade or take action against our NATO allies, we would respond. Same with Japan, same with South Korea, same with Taiwan.'[1] Interpreted as a slip of the tongue at the time, it was taken more seriously a few weeks later, following a CNN town hall meeting in October 2021. Biden was quizzed whether the US would defend Taiwan in the case of invasion. 'Yes, we have a commitment to do that,' he responded.[2] A year after this, talking to CBS News, he re-affirmed the US undertaking. 'Yes, if in fact there was an unprecedented attack,' he said, when asked what the US would do were China to move on Taiwan. The interviewer followed up: 'So unlike Ukraine, to be clear, sir . . . U.S. forces, U.S. men and women would defend Taiwan in the event of a Chinese invasion?' 'Yes,' the president confirmed.[3]

Each time, however, officials from the Biden administration clarified that the One China policy and the doctrine of strategic ambiguity remained unchanged. A White House spokesperson responded to questions about the statements Biden had made by declaring, somewhat mysteriously, that the president had 'made clear then that our Taiwan policy hasn't changed'.[4] This flew in the face of the fact that Biden undoubtedly had said something far stronger than the normal policy position – not once, but three times. It did not help matters, at least in terms of perception by outsiders, that in 2022 a Taiwan Policy Act was passed by the Senate in Washington promising US$4 billion over the ensuing four years in security assistance to the island, and designating it a major non-NATO ally. The legislation also threatened sanctions against Chinese officials found guilty of pressurizing the island.

By 2024, 'strategic ambiguity' and 'defending the status quo' have seemingly decayed to the point of non-existence for Washington. Domestic politics has played a role here: taking a stronger and clearer stand against China more generally is one of the few areas of bipartisan agreement between Democrats and Republicans despite their deep divisions on almost every other policy area. In this environment, speaking in abstractions about abiding by the One China policy, and not spelling out what would happen if Taiwan is threatened, are regarded as acts of appeasement. Many American politicians want to say clearly and categorically how things will unfold, and how they will act, if Beijing *does* make a move. The drift is towards greater and greater candidness.

Even as we acknowledge this new situation, we have to remember that one of the reasons the posture of strategic ambiguity was adopted was because the likely consequences of mishandling this issue and letting it spiral into crisis would be too disastrous to contemplate. The policy was an attempt to manage that risk, ensuring that America maintained its security commitments to Taiwan, but did not get dragged into a scenario which brought it directly into conflict with China. From the time I started dealing with the People's Republic as a student and teacher, in the early 1990s, I realized very quickly that its relations with Taiwan were the most sensitive issue you could bring up with Chinese friends and colleagues. This was never a subject to be flippant and casual about, even with those who were relatively liberal and open-minded.

In the mid-1990s, when the crisis over Chinese military drills in response to the imminent elections in Taiwan occurred, I was based deep in the heart of provincial China, working as a teacher in Hohhot, the capital of the Inner Mongolian region. Each night, as we got closer to the first free and fully democratic presidential plebiscite in Taiwan in March 1996, the state television channel – then called China Central TV – ran denunciations of the main candidate, Lee Teng-hui. His image came to resemble the hated opposition leader in George Orwell's dystopian novel *Nineteen Eighty-Four*. Whenever it came up while I was sitting with friends, I felt almost tangible waves of hatred emanating all around me, inspired by the bespectacled image on the screen. I remember wandering one evening quite late down the main street of Hohhot back to my apartment. There was a roar of lorry engines and, almost from nowhere, a great convoy of green-painted military trucks rolled by. In the back of every one stood soldiers, carrying guns. The whole procession took about ten minutes to pass by. We were so far from the south, from what would have been the main theatre of action if conflict did break out. And yet even here the country seemed on a war footing.

Rumours, and they were always only rumours, spread across Hohhot. People I knew told me – as though they had a direct line to the leadership in Beijing – that China was going to launch an attack against 'the breakaway province'. Lee was a traitor, a splittist, they said. The verbal barrage directed daily against him in the media was relentless. I wondered how the newsreaders didn't go crazy mouthing the same hysterical language, day in and day out, infected by vitriol. But it was only through listening, late at night, to the BBC World Service on shortwave radio (this was long before the internet) that I got a welcome sense of perspective. Conflict was not about to break out, these reports told me. The Chinese fury had in fact been counterproductive, handing Lee a handsome victory in the election. The world could heave a sigh of relief. This was just a war of words, thank goodness. China had sworn Taiwan would never become a democracy – and yet it had become one. Now all the People's Republic could do was get used to it.

The anxiety and fear I briefly felt at this time, followed by the sense of relief when things went back to normal, set a pattern that would repeat over the years ahead. There were moments of intense verbal conflict between Beijing and Taipei, occasions when sabres were rattled, and then a reversion to the brittle, tense but manageable norm. Elections usually served as triggers. The year 2000's was a bad one, because the opposition DPP won, despite Beijing's disfavour and the Chinese state media's attacks. The Chinese premier at the time, Zhu Rongji, threatened in a press conference just before the vote that 'Taiwan independence means war'.[5] Yet the election took place, the DPP won and war didn't break out.

For the near quarter of a century since then, China's aim of reunification has moved further away, rather than any closer. The outside world should not be too self-congratulatory, chalking this up as another victory in a long Cold War Two, where authoritarian China went down to a significant defeat against the free world. Far from Taiwan being allowed to enjoy its own space and behave as it wants today, the net result of all the PRC's setbacks over the last few decades is not resignation and the erosion of its will. What should most worry us is that China's frustration has steadily accumulated even as its objective has remained solidly unchanged. This has fuelled a stronger sense than ever amongst the country's leaders that it needs to act now and assert its claims more urgently.

It is easy to find evidence for this. In his meetings with President Biden in late 2023 at the Asia Pacific Economic Cooperation forum in San Francisco, and in his New Year address for 2024, Xi Jinping repeatedly stated that reunification would happen. 'China will surely be reunified,' he said on the final day of 2023, 'and all Chinese on both sides of the Taiwan Strait should be bound by a common sense of purpose and share in the glory of the rejuvenation of the Chinese nation.'[6] It was merely just a question of when and how. Xi's words are just words – for the moment, at least. But the fact that they are growing more assertive and consistently tougher as time has gone by is clearly no cause for complacency. Nor is Xi alone. When the premier appointed in 2023, Li Qiang, delivered his annual government work report at the National People's Congress in March 2024, it contained a classic statement of the hard and soft approach. 'We [China] will implement our Party's overall policy for the new era on resolving the Taiwan question,' he proclaimed, 'stay committed to the one-China principle and the 1992 Consensus, and resolutely oppose separatist activities aimed at "Taiwan independence" and external interference' – even though he went on to use more placatory language in talking of China being motivated by 'peaceful development' of the cross-strait relationship.[7]

Because of China's tougher position now, it could be argued that America and its allies have no choice but to push back.

They have to make clear to Beijing that any aggressive move on the island will be met with powerful reprisals. With Taiwan under the DPP largely renouncing any notion of unification, either now or in the future, the danger of Taipei exploiting stronger US support to aggressively oppose the mainland's stated designs has increased. Even so, the new worry is not so much about whether the US will stand by Taiwan if attacked – but whether it might proactively recognize Taiwan's sovereignty, and what that might trigger. Here is how this scenario could unfold if we move from words to actions on the Taiwan issue.

Time for Change: America Takes a Stand

Imagine some day in the not-too-distant future that a figure called Senator Brownlow emerges. He is a native of a small town in the US Midwest, but a graduate from Yale and Columbia who worked as a hedge fund manager before going into politics. Since his surprise election to the Senate in 2026 as the authentic voice of flyover America, Brownlow presents himself as champion of the left-behind and neglected, the so-called little people who are ignored by everyone else. A virulent foe of the 'evil Communist empire', as he castigates it in his speeches, Brownlow rails against the way Red China is flooding the US markets with cheap goods, is stealing the country's intellectual property and its manufacturing, and even has the audacity to continue to contest the US-led world order. 'The octogenarians', as Brownlow dubs America's most recent leaders, 'were all talk and no action'. They knew the problems; there was precious little in what he was saying that they would have disagreed with. But they chose to do nothing about it. He clearly has former President Trump in mind: a man who talked big, Brownlow says, and then just lay down and did nothing when the Chinese really pushed back. The senator is standing for president on a platform of being more like Trump than Trump himself. His campaign slogan is 'Others Just Talked, We Will Act'.

Brownlow's harsh words don't just cover fellow politicians. Business people are castigated for greedily filling their pockets with Chinese yuan while selling their own country down the river. 'I am tired,' he says in one address, 'of our generals and top brass saving their skins. I am tired of them doing nothing till they can sit back and collect their pensions. I am tired of listening to their million excuses for inaction.' With American economic decline accelerating, now is the time to do something before it is too late. Decoupling from China and its unfair trade practices has to actually happen rather than continuing to endlessly be debated. America and its allies can go it alone, with no need for China's cheap goods and its markets. It is time for a total disconnect, despite all the gloomy predictions of the so-called experts that the senator clearly loathes.

Brownlow's tone is dramatic, almost apocalyptic when he talks of the imminent struggle between China and the US. At stake, he declares, is nothing less than the future of the whole free world. This is the last stand against Chinese global domination, the moment America's final great battle for freedom and liberty against the darkness of authoritarianism has finally arrived. For eighty years, China's leaders have threatened, postured and blustered. Now he, as President Brownlow, will lead free Americans, the free West, the free world, against the Beijing empire of evil. The crowds love it because of the dramatic way Brownlow presents the US as the global champion of freedom and justice, a place that is restored to its rightful powerful position of the last century as the world's great superpower with no meaningful opponents. A new patriotism binds supporters to his cause. They also love it that he promises to reverse the drain of jobs and dollars to the Chinese corporations that have grown fat at America's expense. Brownlow is heading for a massive victory at the presidential election in November. A man in his mid-forties who has never travelled abroad, who has only ever worked in finance and in provincial domestic politics is poised to take over the world's most powerful nation.

In Beijing, the targets of his rage are busy trying to work out what to make of the new firebrand. He has come from nowhere. There has been no recorded contact with him by any Chinese, including business people or overseas networks. The analysts in the Ministry of Foreign Affairs, preparing their briefing paper for their masters in the Politburo, have to make sense of a man who, going by one interview at least, seems to believe that Singapore is a city in the south of their country and not an independent nation several hours' flight from its coast.

One older advisor says that no one can be this ignorant and ill-informed, and puts these lapses down to mendacity. This man, they claim, is using the ancient method from *The Art of War* by Sun Tzu: trying to appear more idiotic than he actually is in order to disorientate and confuse opponents. But the younger officials aren't so sure. They notice in other statements and speeches by the man most likely to be the new leader of their main foe that China seems to be no more than a symbol for all that is hateful and bad, and that he has a highly black-and-white view of the world. Everyone agrees that things are always like this before elections in the US – so best to reserve judgement. Perhaps, despite everything, pragmatism and business as usual will be restored. Once the drama of campaigning is over, the system will prevail and a little normality will resume.

China, in any case, is distracted by other things. Xi Jinping, in power since 2012, and now seventy-five, has recently been reappointed for a further term as Communist Party leader till 2032 and president till 2033. This is to no one's surprise. But at the congress late the previous year where his party position was announced, everyone observed how the keynote speech usually delivered by him was instead given by Ding Xuexiang, a man who has loyally served Xi since the early 2000s; this March, he was appointed premier, establishing him as the new number two in China's leadership hierarchy. Xi sat on the stage, with a faraway look about him. Rumours of his poor health have been swirling over the first half of the year. During the summer, the hottest ever on record, scorching heat causes tarmac on the roads to melt in some of the southern cities. Floods ravage the vast plateau of the Yellow River causing mass evacuations. Xi disappears for almost a month, leaving Premier Ding and others to do the emergency visits. All that emanates from Beijing are words of concern and comfort on the supreme leader's behalf. When Xi finally emerges in the autumn, greeting old cadres at a Party anniversary, he uses strange language about change coming, things needing rectification, a new wind blowing, and every tree bending before the new forces. 'Maoist' is how one foreigner with a long memory describes it, reminiscent of the final years of the regime's founder in the 1960s and 1970s, when internal fights amongst the elite caused the country to grind to a halt and no one quite knew what was happening.

On the island of Taiwan, at least, there is some stability. At the start of the year, the incumbent president, William Lai

Ching-te of the DPP, was re-elected for a second term of office. Despite a slightly reduced mandate, he was victorious thanks to a divided opposition; the two other contenders shared more than 60 per cent of the vote between them. Lai keeps the independence-supporting faction in his party, and his own deep desire to see the island he leads finally recognized as a state in its own right, under control. But Taiwan's military warns that China is starting to become more active and aggressive, every day sending more and more high-tech jet aircraft deeper and deeper into the island's airspace. There are sporadic brief maritime blockades, imposed like a reminder, an irritant. Nothing major, but they nag at the back of everyone's minds.

And then there are the Americans. For decades, they have stuck to their line, telling Taiwanese leaders to abide by the status quo, despite the odd stray comment from presidents and others saying they will bring the full force of US military might to defend Taiwan if it were ever attacked. After decades of argument and tension, resolution by peaceful means is still the only acceptable approach. Consent by both China and Taiwan before anything can happen is still regarded as crucial. Under all of this lie the fond hopes of a very few either that China would become a liberal democracy, making some sort of unification possible, or that it would simply forget the island and focus on the other, bigger challenges it faces. The Taiwanese know that neither of these is going to happen – at least not in the foreseeable future. Over many years, they have grown to know their so-called compatriots across the strait. Familiarity may not have led to complete contempt, but it has done little to create much in the way of trust. Know your enemy, the ancient Chinese philosophers said, and you can win a thousand battles. Taiwanese know the Chinese. That knowledge has reaffirmed their deep desire to be as separate as possible.

In the last year, however, things have changed. The new generation of American politicians presents a unique problem. The geriatric ones finally shuffling off the stage were a big enough headache, but this emerging group are something else entirely. No constant repetition of how Taiwan must stick with the status quo for them, nor warnings of how the US would never come to the island's aid if it were to try to pre-empt things and provoke China by declaring its full independence. Far from it. Senator Brownlow and his ilk make clear that they intend to follow through on comments by previous politicians such as Mike Pompeo, the former Secretary of State early in the decade, and establish a full diplomatic post in Taipei as a mark of US recognition.

No one has ever seen a situation like this. For as long as anyone can remember, it was the Taiwanese scaring the Americans by being adventurous. Now the Americans are the reckless ones. Senator Brownlow roars one day in a stump speech in Ohio that when he is in the White House the US will reassert its dominant global role and the Taiwanese will get their liberation. America will stick up for them! This figures as part of a powerful narrative about the regeneration and re-affirmation of US power for a major pushback against America's greatest competitor, China. As a precious, free democracy, Taiwan stands on the front line of the global war against the Beijing dictators, he says. The Taiwanese not only can declare their autonomy. They have to. It is now a condition of their alliance with America.

Brownlow has few contacts with officials in the present US administration. He is profoundly antipathetic to what he calls 'the deep state terrorists', bureaucrats running the show with no democratic legitimacy, all part of the whole ugly clump of vested interests he is pledged to destroy. One day, as Brownlow is on his way to address a convention, two State Department officials who happen to be in the building for a different meeting step into the same lift with him. In the couple of minutes that Brownlow is their captive as they ascend to the upper floors, they valiantly try to describe the One China policy that every administration in Washington has adhered to since the early 1970s. Their efforts do not go well. Brownlow accuses them of weasel words and rank sophistry. The encounter seems to have the opposite effect to the one intended. An even harder line on the Taiwan issue now emanates from Brownlow's campaign team.

Another State Department official, going through the friend of a friend of a friend, finally gets to sit down with the senator as he flies from one campaign event to another. She tries to describe the reason for the US's position and the significant issues at stake. She is painstaking in her briefing, saying that Kissinger and Nixon created a framework that has preserved at least a workable peace for more than half a century. 'There are two places that call themselves China,' the official bravely explains, 'but we recognize one.' 'Hey, don't worry,' Brownlow jumps in. 'I only recognize one China too – the empire of evil run by those Commies in Beijing. Taiwan is a free state to me and nothing to do with that.' The official persists: 'Taiwan is regarded as part of the one China, as is the People's Republic, but the administration in reality treats both separately. It is just a form of words.' 'Just a form of words,' the senator mockingly mimics the official. 'Does the world's greatest, freest, mightiest country, a bastion of liberty, let others force words into our mouths? You represent the US government, and you're telling me to capitulate, kowtow, say lies to please others? There are two places. China. Taiwan. Two countries. *That's* my policy.'

This Senator is not for turning. His massive victory in the presidential election, where he carries two thirds of the states and a decisive majority in the electoral college, means that what he has said will happen. He has made it abundantly clear. There will be no rowing back now he is elected. He isn't like all the rest, he says, who threw in the towel the moment they got into office and started producing mealy-mouthed excuses about why they weren't going to do what they'd said they would. Brownlow vows that he is going to be different.

After his inauguration in late January 2029, President Brownlow's first order is to open an official US embassy in Taipei, just as he vowed. He even promises that his first official foreign tour as president will be to Taiwan. He is going to stand by the good people of the island in their fight against the authoritarians. They have nothing to fear. America has their back. It is time someone finally stands up to Beijing and shows them who's still leader of the free world. His speech makes the government in Taiwan go ashen as it listens. And so does its counterpart in Beijing. An American administration conferring legitimacy on Taiwan as a sovereign state, and recognizing its independence, has been the final red line since Beijing and Washington agreed the One China policy six decades ago. That line has now been erased. Beijing must respond and assert its right of ownership over Taiwan. Otherwise it will look like a feeble, passive bystander, afraid to do anything when challenged. That means escalation, the use of its navy and military – and the immediate response of US and Taiwanese forces. Neither China nor the US will back down. The long war of words is now starting to migrate into the world of real force, real weapons. The conflict everyone has feared, and no one has wanted, has finally come into view.

What Would War across the Strait Look Like?

In the recent past, a figure like Senator Brownlow would have belonged to the far reaches of fantasy. But with American politicians in the real world already rehearsing lines that creep towards the positions he espouses, he is no longer so far-fetched. Republican senator Marsha Blackburn, on a visit to Taiwan in 2022, called the place 'a country'. 'We look forward to continuing to help and support Taiwan as they push forward as an independent nation,' she stated, before meeting Tsai Ing-wen.[8] In January 2023, fifteen members of the US House of Representatives led by Republican Tom Tiffany introduced a motion calling on America to formally recognize Taiwan as a state. 'It's time to change the status quo and recognize the reality denied by the United States government for decades: Taiwan is an independent nation,' Tiffany told the media.[9] Six months later, a delegation from the US Republican Study Committee (RSC) led by Kevin Hern reiterated the same point. 'Support for Taiwan as an independent and sovereign nation has been one of the founding principles of the RSC and has remained a top priority for 50 years,' Hern said while they were in Taipei.[10] Currently, these are relatively marginal figures. But the fact that such words of support for something once regarded as taboo are being spoken with greater frequency is ominous. A new paradigm is slowly coming into view where fundamentally questioning the One China policy is now thinkable. It is something that China has consistently condemned and reacted strongly to. The world may be changing. China's position on this issue, however, is definitely not.

Were the US to confer full diplomatic recognition on Taiwan, and were China to launch a retaliatory attack against the island, what might happen? There is not much history to help us answer this question. An account from the last amphibious landing on the island is sometimes cited. But that was in the 1680s, when Qing ships crossed the strait and seized Taiwan. They were facing a small insurgency which was divided and demoralized, operating in a world where primitive muskets or swords and cutlasses were still the favoured weapons. Drawing parallels between then and now is a bit like using descriptions of catching the ferry from Dover to Calais to speculate about how to land on Mars.

Land campaigns in the 2020s – Russia's invasion of Ukraine in 2022, and the Israeli onslaught on Gaza a year later – give some idea of what contemporary battle looks like. Both conflicts have shown that the price in human lives and material infrastructure is colossal. But neither involved crossing a significant stretch of water. In terms of destructiveness, and potential scale, we have never seen a war the way one between China and Taiwan would play out; escalation could bring two nuclear powers, America and the PRC, into direct conflict with each other, along with their unprecedentedly powerful weaponry. But people knowledgeable about military matters paint a uniformly terrifying picture. An authoritative study produced in 2022 in the US warned that 'the military balance between Taiwan and China has shifted decisively in Beijing's favor over the last three decades'.[11] Even so, a full-scale assault culminating in an amphibious landing would not be easy for China. It would take months. China might try to use the greatest weapon any aggressor has at their disposal – surprise. Just as Hamas proved in 2023, with horrific outcomes, simple, low-tech strategies when not expected can bring surprisingly deadly results. Maybe what appears to be a routine military wargame in the strait and surrounding seas suddenly morphs into the real thing. Maybe, while Taiwan and America sleep, the Chinese move in ways too risky to have been predicted and pre-empted. Then everything will be down to snap decisions by a few people, perhaps far away from their political masters in their countries' capitals.

If – or when – the PRC finally makes its move, it could launch cruise missiles at the same time as it deployed crippling cyberattacks. Taiwanese airbases and naval targets, command and control centres, and logistics bases would then all be taken out. In a surprisingly short period of time, the island would be defenceless. As a sign of intent, and of the unexpected depth and detail of their planning, the Chinese could use their vast, new navy to attack US bases in the Pacific, on Guam and Okinawa. Their aim would not be to destroy, however, but to harry, impede and disrupt. China already has plenty of capacity to do this. In the words of the 2022 study quoted above, 'it could employ the entire suite of PLA [People's Liberation Army] capabilities, including electronic warfare, cyber warfare, and information operations. Chinese submarine warfare capabilities and the People's Liberation Army's ability to launch antiship cruise missiles and ballistic missiles from a variety of platforms would greatly complicate Taiwan's defenses.'[12] The tumult that followed might be enough to finally bring home the historic prize: national reunification.

The great German theoretician of conflict from two centuries ago, Carl von Clausewitz, stated in his classic study *On War* that 'war is the realm of chance . . . Chance makes everything more uncertain and interferes with the whole course of events.'[13] Things happen with a speed way beyond the everyday norm. People do not have time to think. No matter how much they have prepared and practised, in the end it is instinct that actors in the field of conflict fall back on, rather than even the most rudimentary deliberation. The aggressor has the initial advantage: they at least know the first move, even if they don't know precisely how things will unfold after that. China knows it would face vast imbalances in any fight against the US. But it also knows that the US would need to cope with the distance that separates it from the theatre of operations. For China, Taiwan is 130 kilometres away. For the US, its naval assets would need to cover multiples of that distance, from Guam or Okinawa. How quickly they could do this might make the difference between victory and defeat.

It is very likely that Chinese forces would impose a blockade to isolate Taiwan, barring sea lanes to prevent America and its allies from coming, cutting off supplies to the island, and severing the internet. While this took place, the navy and air force of the People's Liberation Army would have to carry out amphibious and airborne assaults on a scale not seen since the Second World War. 'An invasion would require a massive mobilization of PLA forces, equipment, and logistics capabilities,' the American 2022 report states:

> The first phase would involve efforts to degrade Taiwan's air and naval defenses in preparation for an amphibious assault. The PLA would utilize precision ballistic and cruise missile strikes against Taiwan's air and missile defenses, precision long-range artillery, airstrikes with medium-range bombers and fighters, and antiship cruise missile and submarine attacks against Taiwan's naval assets. Taiwan would employ its air and missile defense and air force and naval assets to defend targets and contest PLA efforts to gain maritime and air superiority. The PLA would then need to execute an amphibious assault to establish a beachhead on Taiwan and an airborne/air assault attack to try to seize an airfield and a port facility that could

allow the PLA to use civilian transportation assets to provide air and sea lift. The PLA would then have to land sufficient ground combat forces to defeat Taiwan's ground forces and provide sufficient ammunition, fuel, and other supplies to support these forces during combat operations.[14]

Strategic thinkers argue that, as of early 2024, China is not in a position to undertake such a landing because it lacks the technology and firepower. It is clear, though, that if it did get a large enough contingent of troops on to the island, we would enter a new, unprecedented phase. Then it would be down to the people of Taiwan themselves to mount any opposition to the invaders.

A domestic war of resistance would begin. The situation at that point might resemble the Russian war against Ukraine. The PLA would try to bomb cities such as Taipei and Kaohsiung, vast places with millions of inhabitants. It would try to degrade the island's defensive capacity and destroy its infrastructure, such as its bridges and high-speed rail. It would also continue to prevent food, fuel and other materials reaching the island with its huge naval and air blockade. Its aim would be to force the Taiwanese political leadership to make a simple decision: capitulate and survive? Or fight and perish? If any conflict across the strait reached this stage, it would already be too late for a negotiated compromise and a return to the status quo. Beijing would need to win; it would go down if it failed to do so. Even the least disastrous outcome would have world-changing consequences.

And then there are the global ramifications that would kick into action the moment it became clear what China was intending to do. There would be immediate crisis meetings. The UN Security Council would go into overdrive. American and

European politicians would need to make split-second decisions about what their response might be. We have seen that a cross-strait conflict wouldn't just be a geopolitical event. It would also aim a dagger at the heart of the global economy, causing an instantaneous crash in global stocks, and slashing a hole in the middle of supply chains and trade flows. One estimate has put the immediate baseline impact on global GDP at US$2 trillion.[15] A veteran of the microchip industry in Taiwan, Miin Wu, speaking in June 2023, said that conflict would set back the global economy 'at least 20 years'.[16] At the very least, a severe recession, and more probably a steep global depression, would be the outcome. The world's supply of high-tech superconductors to power its most crucial computers and robots would abruptly stop. That alone, as the temporary disruption due to COVID-19 in 2020–21 demonstrated, would have a dramatic impact. Anyone that wishes to play around with the Taiwan issue – whether they're Chinese, Taiwanese or from the rest of the world – has to realize that these dystopian scenarios are not on the outer edges of possibility. On the contrary, they are highly likely. Chinese conflict with Taiwan would remake the world, leaving behind it a planet that is poorer and even more profoundly divided than it is at present.

Contemplating real conflict between China and Taiwan, rather than the war of words, gestures and speculation that so far we have lived amidst, involves thinking through a whole set of tough issues concerning the extent to which the West would stand by the island, and the price it might be willing to pay to do so. Anyone can utter grand-sounding security promises and strong protestations of support before an attack actually happens. Then, once it has occurred, the initial resolve can be worn down quite quickly. The Russian invasion of Ukraine in

2022 was met at first with impressive unity and purposefulness by the US and its allies. Sanctions were imposed and Russia was frozen out of the international finance system. For the first year, these bit into Russia's domestic economy. Military assistance was offered to Ukraine, including technology, equipment and financial support. But as 2023 wore on, fatigue set in. The US Congress refused to approve the budget for future assistance at the end of 2023, only finally voting it through several months later. The world was further distracted by the eruption of conflict between Israel and Palestine after terrorist attacks carried out by Hamas from Gaza on 7 October 2023. It became even more vexed when Iran launched a massive missile and aerial drone attack on Israel in April 2024, which threatened to ignite conflict across the Middle East.

Yet a war instigated by China with Taiwan would have repercussions many times greater than those of the Russia–Ukraine situation or the Israel–Iran one, however grave we rightly view these to be. Russia's economy is only a small percentage of the size of China's. Its military is large, but nowhere near as well-funded as that of China. The only advantage it has is combat experience in recent years, something China lacks. A land war too is a different matter to one involving amphibious operations, for the simple reason that it is easier to move military equipment and troops on the ground, where they are less vulnerable to air attack than they are when crammed into ships at sea. Finally, Russia had already been isolated to some extent from the global economic system by the time it attacked Ukraine in 2022. China and Taiwan sit at the heart of that system. In a scenario where the global economy is already groaning under pressure, and where electorates are expressing greater and greater discontent with their daily living standards, the will to support Taiwan and stand by it may end up being far weaker than expected. We just won't know until it is actually tested.

What we do know is that a conflict across the strait, one involving a sustained blockade or military action up to and including a full-scale attempted invasion, would represent the most elemental ideological clash. It would be one where the values of the democratic world face those of its most formidable authoritarian opponent. This endows the issue of Taiwan with global importance. It is not just about the fate of one small island state with a middle-sized economy and a relatively modest population. It is about political and economic issues that profoundly matter across the rest of the world, ones that will shape the future global order. Taiwan is the place where China and the US, the two dominant powers of our age, face off against each other, not just over the question of raw power, but over whose ideas and values have the most potency and validity in the twenty-first century. An invasion of Taiwan would raise the terrifying question of just how much the outside world would do to defend its principles – or whether it no longer has the capacity, the self-belief or the willpower to do so.

8. Thinking Through the Future: The Taiwan Challenge in the Twenty-first Century

Predictions of an imminent clash between Taiwan and China are not new. What is worrying today is that the claims of looming conflict across the strait are becoming more frequent, the time frame shorter – and the people making these assertions not just commentators or spectators, but significant military or political figures.

In January 2023, General Mike Minihan, a former senior commander of US forces in the Indo-Pacific region, stated that America and China would 'fight' over Taiwan by 2025.[1] The Taiwanese Minister of National Defence, Chiu Kuo-cheng, speaking to members of the Legislative Assembly on 7 March 2024, repeated a claim he had first made in 2021 that the region was on the brink of war. While some dismissed his comments as hyperbole, they underlined a sense of urgency building up like a pressure cooker.[2] In just the first two months of 2024 alone, respected media outlets such as Reuters, *Foreign Policy*, Bloomberg and *Politico* all carried articles speculating about how imminent conflict might be and the likely outcomes.[3] With discussions like these swirling around in the general awareness, it seems almost as if the first stage of the fight has already started. The phoney war is underway; it's only a matter of time before the real one kicks off.

Many of these reports were clear-sighted about the disastrous consequences of conflict. The *New York Times* in October

2023 declared that 'a war between the United States and China over Taiwan could be the most brutal since World War II'.[4] Analyst Robert A. Manning, writing in January 2024, stated: 'Short of a nuclear war, a conflict over Taiwan would unquestionably cause catastrophic economic damage, not only for the United States and mainland China but for the rest of the world.'[5] So while there was still some disagreement over whether a war would happen, and how it might pan out if it started, there was broad consensus that any conflict would be serious, and that all involved would suffer calamity. That at least hinted at the imperative for all parties to show some restraint.

Despite this widespread acceptance, it is a lugubrious fact that history is full of wars that no one intended, which made very little sense logically, but which still happened. The First World War is a much studied example, a devastating conflict which cost millions of lives, and which was partly due to the build-up of an alliance system that committed countries to declaring war once a treaty partner was embroiled in a fight, and partly to competition among European states in the decades at the turn of the twentieth century. Stumbling accidentally into a huge war from an initially small incident offers possible parallels with the situation in the early twenty-first-century Asia Pacific region, ones that have been noted not just by academics and commentators but by high-level Asian policymakers. The late Shinzo Abe, when Prime Minister of Japan, stated at a conference in 2014 that the situation between China and Japan was 'similar' to Britain and Germany before 1914, when their excellent economic links did not prevent the outbreak of hostilities between them.[6] His spokesperson afterwards rowed back from the statement. But the underlying insight that there were tensions across the region that could ineluctably lead to implosion resonated with the possibility that a Chinese move on Taiwan would be the event to detonate it.

What are the options for managing Taiwan's status in order to avoid history repeating itself with a potentially far worse version of the First World War, this time involving nuclear weapons with their almost limitless capacity for destruction? Do we have to prepare for a future where it is a choice between appeasing the PRC's demands, and a full-on confrontation over an island of 23 million people? What real scope do we have to act to ensure this issue doesn't end up being the war that no one wanted and everyone feared, but which broke out all the same? One of the key things we can all do is adopt a more realistic context within which to view the challenge of managing Taiwan's status. It is patently clear that whatever solutions there might be in the long term – whether independence or unification or something in between – the conditions do not exist at present to achieve any of them without a high risk of disaster. We need to adjust our thinking to accept this. What follows therefore is a realist, pragmatic proposal. It is more about an approach than about identifying a single, straightforward solution. It is based on acceptance, on managing the situation as it is, rather than on hopeful aspirations about what it might become.

To start off, we need to look at the fundamentals of the current impasse. Three factors in particular have made management of the Taiwan issue more urgent and more challenging since 1980. They have been spelled out in this book. The first is a bold and confident China that has dramatically grown its economy and its military, has become more nationalistic, and has developed a far greater capacity than ever before to try to achieve its regional ambitions. The second is a Taiwan increasingly convinced of the right to exist on its own terms after undergoing democratization since the 1980s, and possessing a younger generation with little if any sense of connection to the mainland, either socially or culturally. The third is a West led by a United States threatened and angered by the major challenge to its global power of China (and by others, such as Russia), but beset by internal divisions and troubles and by dwindling self-confidence.

The intensification of these three factors is what makes this problem so incendiary today, and has led to the increased talk of war. Even a decade ago, they were not yet as acute as they are now. As they grate against each other, frustration amongst all the parties continues to mount. In order to address the Taiwan challenge, the world needs to focus on how to manage each of these three factors, and recognize that if they continue to grow, the chances of a real conflict breaking out increases. All sides need to accept that we may not be able to cool down the issue, but we can at least allow it to simmer rather than bringing it catastrophically to the boil.

The Options

Much thought by scholars, analysts and policymakers has gone into mapping out how the challenge of Taiwan's status might be managed without a disaster occurring. At one end of the chart are the roads to unification proffered by Beijing. Those who claim to take a wider view, and who promote a version of 'leave Asia to the major Asian power, China', suggest that the outside world tolerate bolder Chinese action towards Taiwan in return for more cooperative relations elsewhere. At the other end of the map are various routes to the peaceful acceptance of Taiwan's independence. Perhaps most striking is the idea of establishing a federal 'United States of China', as proposed by the political scientist Scott Moore amongst others, who argued in the *New York Times* in 2014 that 'federalism represents the only conceivable, peaceful long-term solution to Beijing's nagging problem of Taiwan'.[7]

On the face of it, the notion of a federation looks possible. Not counting Taiwan, China currently comprises thirty-three provincial-level entities: the twenty-two provinces themselves; five autonomous regions such as Tibet; four municipalities with higher status, such as Beijing; and the two special administrative regions, Hong Kong and Macau. All have some degree of autonomy in terms of the budgets they can set and the ways they administer themselves. The idea of a looser system holding together the separate parts of the vast entity that is China, therefore, is not an alien one. Taiwan could figure in this arrangement, sharing the same brand, but able to run its internal affairs with almost total freedom. A federation along these lines, if it could be made to work, would remove much of the present security challenge and create stability. Its great advantage is that it accepts a connection between either side of the strait, but it stops short of granting complete sovereignty and control to Beijing. It grants Taiwan some distinctive space for expressing and exercising its autonomy. China would operate like a holding company, and Taiwan as a largely free and separate subsidiary.

The main obstacles to its possibility today are the resolute opposition from Beijing and rejection by the majority of Taiwanese themselves. The government of Xi Jinping regards any role for federalism in the future governance of China with deep suspicion, and does not believe its 'One Country, Two Systems' policy contains any space for federal thinking. The Xi era has been a centralizing one, with fiscal and budgetary powers increasingly exercised by the central government in Beijing. The greatest issue, however, is how granting broader freedoms to some provinces might stir similar desires in Tibet, Xinjiang or anywhere else in the country with a high proportion of ethnic minorities and a history of desiring greater autonomy. For all Beijing's assertiveness abroad, there is an intrinsic vulnerability to China's domestic condition, caused by a visceral fear of fragmentation and break-up. This was, after all, something that had occurred almost within living memory, during the chaotic 1920s–1940s, when the country was carved up into separate zones and fiefdoms. Tolerating a federal deal with Taiwan would potentially open a can of worms in relation to the integrity of China's borders, and that is not something Beijing is willing to risk. Taiwan too would be highly unlikely to regard federation with the mainland as anything other than the thin end of the wedge – a deal which would slowly be eroded, and which runs counter to its own desire for autonomy. Nor could it even start to contemplate such an arrangement without China politically changing first, and becoming a democracy.

Right at the other end of the scale of possibilities is the realpolitik strategy, which has been advocated by Australian academic Hugh White. In his hard-headed view, the world must accept that in any conflict over Taiwan China would prevail. Writing in 2016, he stated, 'China is simply too important economically, and too powerful militarily, for anyone to confront it on Taiwan's behalf, especially when everyone knows how determined China is to achieve reunification eventually.' He continued:

reality does not yet seem to have sunk in in Washington, where leaders still talk boldly about their willingness to stand by

Taiwan without seriously considering what that might mean in practice. Any US effort to support Taiwan militarily against China would be almost certain to escalate into a full-scale US–China war and quite possibly a nuclear exchange. That would be a disaster for everyone, including, of course, the people of Taiwan itself – far worse than unification, in fact.[8]

White argues that the outside world must be pragmatic and accept that China has a far larger legitimate role to play in the region around it, driven by its fears of vulnerability in places such as the South and East China Seas. From this perspective, Taiwan is merely one piece in a wider picture rather than the sole decisive detail. In order to avoid China feeling fractious, frustrated and penned in, and making itself troublesome to the wider world, an agreement should be reached. China would be granted more latitude to exercise control over neighbouring regions, giving it the greater security that it craves. In exchange, it would accept a far more consensual, multilateralist role outside this core sphere. The main objective for the international community would be to support Taiwan in negotiating as advantageous a position within China as possible, which could be sold to Taiwanese as providing the stability and security that they currently lack.

Needless to say, White's approach has been fiercely criticized, both on the grounds of seeming to appease China for aggressive and bellicose behaviour, and for underestimating how making concessions would encourage China to pursue aims further afield – precisely the opposite effect to the one intended.[9] On top of this, it seems to disregard the most important aspect of the Taiwan challenge – the ways in which it involves the defence not just of a location but of a set of values. If the US and its democratic allies backed down over

Taiwan, it would be much more than a regional matter. It would have global, and historic, ramifications. Symbolically, it would be read as democracy caving in to authoritarianism. That would be a paradigm shift. One that would have profound and far-reaching political and ideological implications, rather than merely territorial ones.

The 'Steady State' Approach

Alongside these options, other analysts have invited all the key players to stand back, take a deep breath, and survey the current situation with at least some attempt at calm objectivity. They emphasize that everyone is likely to end up a loser in any conflict, in a China–Taiwan version of mutually assured destruction. Their proposals instead aim to persuade the chief participants – China, Taiwan and the US and its allies – to try to create a new, manageable conceptual framework to work within. The main question they address is where the players should focus their attention.

The respected International Crisis Group think tank, in a report issued in 2023, took a largely political approach. It urged both Washington and Beijing of the need to restore confidence in each other, and to de-escalate the tensions that had risen over the previous few years. The report argued that 'Washington should turn over a new leaf with respect to its implementation of the "one China" policy – becoming more disciplined and eschewing loud, symbolic actions that are unnecessary and ultimately more costly than beneficial to Taiwan.' In turn, 'Beijing must understand that shows of military force may reinforce a sense in Taiwan that formal independence would be disastrous.' The report continued, 'If the mainland truly wants to preserve a peaceful unification option, Beijing would have to move beyond muscle flexing, instead increasing the attractiveness of the model it is offering to Taiwanese.'[10] Enhancing US–China dialogue, ensuring that there is top-level discussion both with and about Taiwan, and working hard to remove potential causes of mutual misunderstanding and rebuild trust, are the group's main recommendations for a more 'dynamic' environment for cross-strait relations.

These ideas align to some degree with those of the American experts Richard Bush, Bonnie Glaser and Ryan Hass, who have also focused on the idea of keeping the problem in proportion. They have argued that over-hyping the threat China poses to Taiwan ends up doing Beijing's work for it by making everyone else timid and unwilling to confront it for fear of things getting out of hand. As a way beyond this panicky attitude, they propose a broader approach: 'If American policy makers want to help Taiwan, they will need to go beyond focusing on the military threat,' they state. The US–Taiwan economic relationship has to be upgraded and modernized so that it can help Taiwan diversify its trade ties and give it more opportunities to feel respected and that it has agency.[11] This is a worthy idea, but in the one area where the US does value and recognize Taiwanese capabilities – advanced semiconductor manufacturing – it has insisted since 2023 that more of the production is done in America, for security reasons.[12]

Each of these options – the federal solution; the 'grand deal' accepting short-term sacrifices for longer-term benefits; the enhancing and diversifying of economic links and outside support – map out very different lines of approach. Viewed together, they demonstrate just how little consensus there is on how to tackle the issue of Taiwan. In particular, the world is no longer as unified as it once was on the One China policy, and there is less agreement than ever before on how fit for purpose its framework is. That in itself is fundamental, because it is precisely where misunderstanding and miscommunication might occur. It could be the spark that ignites the powder keg. As with the First World War, no one intended things to escalate, and yet enough signs were misread and enough intentions were misunderstood for that to finally happen.

Finding Ways Forward

One new way to think about the current situation is to accept the fact of stalemate and regard it not as a negative, but a positive thing. Despite Beijing's ambitions and motives, the impediments to achieving them (international condemnation, the risk of global war, economic collapse and massive internal opposition in Taiwan) are still daunting. Despite Taiwan's desire for the greater freedom and autonomy that will lead to independence, the awareness that trying to achieve this would almost certainly prompt Beijing to take drastic action applies a powerful brake and stops the island from taking the risk. And despite the US and its allies' desire for clarity and for what they see as Taiwan's just treatment, the price for supporting the island too overtly could be to risk smashing apart the global economic and security systems at a time when they are already under enough pressure elsewhere. Ironically, as long as the current situation persists, a stalemate is the only option which will not precipitate an outright crisis. After all, that has broadly been the status quo for the last few decades.

What unites the three main players is their common desire for security. China may seem to want reunification principally for emotional and nationalistic reasons, but at the heart of that sits a strong desire for protection. It wants validation as a great power of the twenty-first century, for sure, but the reason for that is the sense of stability and safety it gives the country. People are less likely to launch an attack on a strong, dominant power than on a weaker, fragmented one. Taiwan wants autonomy because it feels it is a separate place now, and because the values and governance of China are a threat to its way of life and to its own survival; the more independent it is, the better it can mitigate against this. The US and the West want a stable Asia, and a China and Taiwan that are both dependable and less antagonistic, neither of whom will launch an attack across the strait or contend with each other in ways that are destabilizing for everyone else. For all three, the desire for security and stability is perhaps the only point they have in common.

Where they differ is how best to achieve this aim. China is currently convinced that the ideal guarantee would be a reunited country (regardless of whether that has much basis in historical reality) with everyone happily belonging to one great national entity. Taiwan desires to be free of threat by having autonomy and being accepted for what it is, rather than being forced to conform to someone else's idea of what it should be. The US and the West have faith that the ideals of democracy and individual freedom are the best route to harmony and an enduring global order. The core conundrum, however, is that by each separately aiming for what they believe is the key to their security, they are in fact achieving the precise opposite. China claiming Taiwan, or Taiwan declaring independence, or the US and the West recognizing that independence – any of these could bring about the conflagration described in the previous chapter.

The Times They are a-Changin'

We need to recognize that the differences between China, Taiwan and the US and its allies over how to achieve security are currently insurmountable. But that does not mean we have to accept the current stalemate as an endpoint. Rather, it has to be understood as a holding pattern, something to be preserved until the overall situation changes. Underneath the Taiwan challenge, there run deep-rooted strata that will determine this.

The tectonic fault lines which impel the island's current situation are sovereignty and identity, and the attitudes defining them. The ways these are now configured help us understand why the Taiwan issue is insoluble today. But it is through them that the chance for change and transformation will occur in the longer term. And only when that happens will there be any space for other, better outcomes.

Questions of sovereignty and identity shape not just the problem of Taiwan's status but almost all of global politics today. In different ways, they are the engine for some of the most passionate debates in Europe and the US as well as Asia. In the South and East China Seas, states such as Vietnam, the Philippines, Malaysia and Japan argue over territorial disputes to the verge of conflict. The conflict between Russia and Ukraine is driven by territorial claims relating to wider themes of national identity and status, notably the former's notion that it is striving to restore a historic greater Russian state. And the almost endless animosity between Israel and the Palestinian Authority can be explained by both demanding sole control over lands with which they both feel a profound historic bond.

The prime importance of sovereignty for national security

in East and Southeast Asia is interesting, because it shows how subject to change these kinds of huge, underlying structural issues are. Historically, the idea of set boundaries between entities called 'states' was an alien one for many in this region. Chinese dynasties in the past had only an abstract notion of what constituted a political unit with control over its own affairs, and it did not feature the sense of clearly marked physical borders. Sinologists in the last century, such as John K. Fairbank and Lucian Pye, and many scholars in China today, such as Ge Zhaoguang, have argued that China was distinctive because it regarded itself as a civilization, a zone of cultural influence which gradually faded over distance, rather than as a state with a fixed, clear-cut boundary to mark the limits of its authority.[13]

Despite this, the notion of sovereignty and the idea of nation states, as they evolved from the 1648 Treaty of Westphalia in Europe, have been two of the most successful political exports from the West to Asia. This is partly because so many of the states across the region suffered colonization in one form or another in the modern era, China included. Their current shape was often dictated by the interference of powers like the Netherlands, France and Britain. Indonesia, Singapore, the Philippines and Malaysia all underwent struggles to build the national consciousness necessary for ridding themselves of their colonizers and existing as independent entities. To this end, the idea of nations possessing autonomy within internationally recognized and respected borders – strongly implicit within the Western concept of sovereignty – proved very attractive. Hence the passionate commitment to national sovereignty found in the region to this day. Multilateralism is weak and the notion of pooled sovereignty along the lines of the European Union unfamiliar. By contrast, the Association of

Southeast Asian Nations is amongst the world's weakest international regional cooperative bodies. Countries are rigorous in the protection and defence of their national autonomy because of the ways they felt these were violated in the past.

Since the establishment of its current regime in 1949, China has stood amongst the most insistent Asian countries on the issue of sovereignty. This is particularly because it has made national self-determination and opposition to foreign colonialism two of the key pillars of its legitimacy. It has embraced the principle that the nation state comprises the most important unit of global governance with almost obsessive passion. In 1982, when Deng Xiaoping met with British Prime Minister Margaret Thatcher for initial discussions over the future of Hong Kong once British control ended in 1997, he vigorously rejected her proposal that Britain might continue to help administer the territory after that date. As he explained, sovereignty was non-negotiable, and not to be shared – particularly with a power so closely associated by Chinese with foreign interference in its internal affairs in the past.

Despite this, there are times when this cast-iron, rigid notion of sovereignty has been treated more flexibly by the PRC. Hong Kong is a case in point. Despite Deng's fierce words to Thatcher, it was initially allowed greater autonomy, with the prospect of keeping its own system of governance and its capitalist economy for another fifty years, until 2047. China has also been pragmatic about sovereignty in its border negotiations with several neighbours, from the 1960s through to the 2000s. It has, for instance, been prepared to cede territory to the Russians and Vietnamese in order to ensure stability and certainty.

The question now is just how much China's attitude towards sovereignty might change in the coming decades. Under Xi

Jinping, its stand has been hardline. Tibet, Xinjiang, Hong Kong, Macau, Inner Mongolia are all seen as part of a great unified, centralized entity. They are to be led uniformly by the Communist Party in Beijing, and are to share equally in its vision of a rejuvenated Chinese state. But there are global perils looming – macroeconomic upheaval, the effects of climate change, future pandemics – where sovereignty will have to be modified or rethought if they are to stand any chance of being addressed. Like all countries in the era of global trade, China has assumed a more transactional stance on at least some forms of economic and regulatory control, accepting convergence with international standards and agencies (such as the World Trade Organization, which it joined in 2001). It has adopted some common standards of accounting for carbon emissions and engages with the UN's climate change forum (COP). This shows that at least where self-interest is strong enough, China can and does compromise. Its expressions of sovereignty are not absolute or eternal, but on a spectrum. It is just a question of where and when it is willing to draw the line.

China's uncompromising attitude at present to sovereignty is the key reason why it has shown no flexibility on Taiwan – or, for that matter, on Hong Kong, or on other issues relating to its territory. Its mindset is that its national security can be preserved only by complete intransigence. But this has, in fact, led to greater resistance from Taiwan and, indeed, from the US. Paradoxically, the key argument that needs to be put to Beijing is that if its core aim is to ensure stability and make one-party rule sustainable, the surest way of jettisoning that ambition would be to attack Taiwan. China's security is best safeguarded by a looser approach to sovereignty, not a tighter one.

Sitting next to sovereignty on the deep structural fault lines running under the Taiwan issue is identity. The first chapter of this book spelled out how far notions of identity have changed both on the mainland and on the island over the last few decades. Were we dealing with two partners bonded by a powerful commonality of values and culture, and by a shared world view, then the path to solutions would be far easier to trace. But at the moment, what we have instead are two populations with very different senses not only of what makes them who they are, but also of what they share and how they are connected. And it seems to be getting more pronounced as time goes on.

Identity politics afflicts communities everywhere. The so-called culture wars since the 1960s in America and elsewhere in the West typify this. Groups settle on a common language and symbols that bind them together, and then they clash with other groups adhering to other languages and symbols – over issues such as the legal right to abortion, the space permitted marginalized groups in society, or how to define key aspects of gender and religion. Identity is a battleground because it is underpinned by powerful political, cultural, religious and ethnic dynamics that involve the most sensitive and contentious strands of any society. Creating some sort of consensus takes vast effort and patience. If these differences are allowed to run out of control, clashes over identity can rip societies apart.

Yet identity, self-evidently, can be plastic and mutable. The solidifying of Taiwanese identity has been as much about the need to face down the threat and coercion of China as it has been about the impact on society of the growing economy and the rise of democracy. Today, Taiwanese have evolved ways of reconciling at least some conflicts about who people believe they are and what they want from their society. The Sunflower

Movement's 2014 protests were a moment when powerful oppositional forces clashed with each other, and contention came out into the open. Compromise, negotiation and consensus-building through civic groups and political organizations helped to defuse the crisis. The government listened to criticism and backed down, and the opposition groups called off their protests. But today, between young and old, between straight and gay, between the well-off and the less privileged, Taiwan is as fractured and riven with different viewpoints as any other society. That it has the freest media in Asia, according to most surveys, allows everyone both inside and outside the island to see this. So to claim that Taiwanese identity is rock-solid and immutable would be nonsense. After all, it has changed markedly in the last thirty years – and it will continue to do so.

The same can be said of Chinese identity, though there the evidence is harder to find. The protests at the end of 2022 against the harsh COVID-19 lockdowns were one of the rare recent signs of social fracturing and discontent. Other research has shown how diverse attitudes and self-identity are in the country. The greatest division is probably between old and young, thanks to the impact of phenomena such as the One Child policy from the 1980s, which has created a generation who have had far more privileges than their parents and grandparents, and today have far higher expectations. China has transformed more dramatically than many other societies since 1949. It is a place that has often been afflicted with rapid and disorientating change. Only someone brave or foolhardy would predict how Chinese might see themselves and define their fundamental values in the coming decades.

Chinese self-perception and self-belief, and the ways in which Chinese regard the country's culture, will be enormously important for determining the future status of Taiwan. China's attitude towards Taiwan comes across as coercive and intolerant, accepting only a very narrow definition of what it means to be Chinese and of how Chinese culture can be shared. Paradoxically yet again, the more extreme that nationalism becomes on either side of the strait, and the greater the role it plays in defining Chinese or Taiwanese identity, the less likely it is that the Taiwan issue will ever be resolved without courting the sort of catastrophe described earlier. A more flexible sense of national identity offers at least some potential pathways to a solution.

The situation regarding neither of these two underlying structural issues – sovereignty and identity – looks remotely encouraging at the moment. But if there is ever to be a sustainable settlement of the Taiwan issue, it will be because of developments in these two areas. In neither area is the current Chinese or Taiwanese position set in stone. The simple fact is that, for either side to achieve any of their goals, both of them will need to revise their current approach. Like it or not, the rest of the world needs to accept that the road to peace for Taiwan runs through Beijing. And while flexibility on both sides will be essential, the position of the People's Republic is the more important one, because it is the Beijing government that is currently demanding a change to the status quo.

Being Responsible

As of today, however, we live with tensions, uncertainty and what looks like a looming crisis. No new thinking in Beijing seems to be emerging on the great issues of sovereignty and identity, nor does it look like any will be forthcoming in the near future. The only workable approach at the moment is management, containment and constant restraint. For this to be achievable, all the key parties in the Taiwan issue have a role to play.

For the Americans and their alliance system, the greatest danger comes from regarding Taiwan as the great frontier where the final fight between authoritarianism and freedom will take place. Writing in an article for *Foreign Affairs* magazine in April 2024, US Congressman Mike Gallagher – former chairman of the House Select Committee on the Chinese Communist Party – and former US Deputy National Security Advisor Matt Pottinger pictured the rivalry between the two superpowers as akin to a great game, before declaring that 'the United States shouldn't manage the competition with China; it should win it'. They adamantly asserted that 'Xi is preparing his country for a war over Taiwan' and that 'the only path to avoid this future is for Washington to immediately build and surge enough hard power to deny Xi a successful invasion'.[14]

This is dangerous zero-sum thinking, at a dangerous time. Pottinger and Gallagher situate the Taiwan issue as part of a vast cultural and ideological clash between the US and China, where the only conceivable outcome for either great power is supremacy over the other. There is no awareness in this sort of argument that using the island as a proxy to push back against what the US defines as the key threat of Chinese power does not necessarily align with Taiwan's best interests or Taiwanese views. It could be the fastest route to conflict, not the best strategy for global security. Defending Taiwan's right to the principle of self-determination is all well and good. But figuring it as the best opportunity for the US and the West's final showdown with China does not serve the interests of anyone, not least those who would receive the brunt of the inevitable repercussions – the people of Taiwan. Instead of this approach, Taiwan's dispute with China needs to be set outside the arena of superpower contention, the way it was when the One China policy was created in the 1970s. It needs to be understood as nothing more than a disagreement between the two parties directly involved, who need to accept that no coercion or force should be used by one side against the other to bring about a resolution. Everything that is done must be peaceful, and meet with consensus and mutual agreement. In that way, the West can preserve its neutrality, and maintain at least some degree of credibility with both parties, allowing it to bring its influence to bear on either side of the argument.

The importance of sanity and restraint need to be impressed on China too. The economic, social and political costs of forcing a resolution on Taiwan need to be kept in mind every hour of every day. Provocations by outside actors, and occasionally by Taiwan itself, need to be seen for what they are – attempts to rile and stir up China rather than constructive solutions. Those that engage with China on this issue – whether as politicians, diplomats or academics – need to reinforce at every step that no matter where they stand on the rightness or otherwise of China's ultimate aims, even the most benign outcome of a Chinese attempt to resolve the status of Taiwan without Taiwanese consent would lead to catastrophe. China is a self-interested power, one whose people have made huge sacrifices to rebuild and redefine their country over the last century. Taiwan might have immense symbolic and emotional importance for them, but it is also the one issue most likely to cause everything that the PRC has worked for to disappear in gigantic swathes of smoke and fire. Eventually, China will need to evolve a more creative conception of the great structural issues of sovereignty and identity. But it will need time – and now is not the moment to force that.

For the Taiwanese, the task is even more urgent and complex. Managing the great powers bearing down on them is a vast enough job. But the Taiwanese need to always bear in mind the lessons of their own recent history. The US relationship is crucial, but it is not – and has never been – wholly dependable. America undertook dramatic changes in its policy on Taiwan in the 1970s; its support today might look solid and have some legal basis, but that could quickly change. The volatility of US internal politics is an increasing worry for everyone. Taiwan needs to be wary of engaging with adventurist politicians driven more by their own domestic agenda than a sincere desire to contribute to the sustainable management of the island's situation.

Dialogue in a context as sensitive as this, where the stakes if things go wrong are so high, is critical. The lack of top-level engagement between the island and China since 2016 is a serious problem. That it might continue under the DPP with their new president in 2024, William Lai Ching-te, is also concerning. It is unthinkable that there might be no significant contact at senior level between the two parties for more than a decade. This is especially so because the real decision-making circle in China is extremely small. It centres on Xi Jinping and his coterie of key advisors, the most important of whom, on Taiwan matters, is his chief ideologue, Wang Huning. There are constant worries about how well informed and up to date elite Chinese leaders are on issues relating to Taiwan, and what sort of information or intelligence gets fed to them. (This is despite the fact that, for the first time in many decades, there is a member of the seven-man inner Standing Committee of the Politburo, Cai Qi, who has actually visited Taiwan, albeit back in 2012, some years before his elevation.)

Clearly, former president Ma Ying-jeou was right in trying to maintain this sort of contact in his latest meeting with Xi Jinping in April 2024. But he is no longer regarded by the current government in Taipei as an interlocutor with any credibility. That does not invalidate what he was trying to achieve, however. A new figure who has standing in Taipei, Beijing and Washington – potentially a special emissary – needs to be identified and appointed. They can at least be a conduit for the exchange of essential information and ideas.

But Taiwan and China need to find broader ways to speak to each other beyond diplomatic ones. The travel, collaboration and communication between ordinary people that were disrupted by China's hostile reaction to the election of the DPP to power in 2016, and then by the impact of the COVID-19 pandemic, need to be nurtured again. As does cultural dialogue across the strait. The numbers of students from Taiwan studying in China, and vice versa, plummeted during the pandemic. So too did the numbers of tourists and business visitors. Effort must go into building these forms of interchange up again. They at least provide a modest means for the two sides to understand each other a little, even if they don't and won't agree about much.

Beyond the practical matter of direct contact, particularly at the highest levels, there is the issue of establishing a framework for dialogue which is based on at least some degree of commonality, however abstract and non-committal. The fiction of the 1992 Consensus, where both sides agreed that there was one China but interpreted differently precisely what that meant, had at least some value. It created the mirage that there was a minimal degree of common ground between the two that they might work within. But the DPP have refused to recognize it since 2016, following Tsai Ing-wen's election as president. While perfectly understandable on a political level, it has served as a constant impediment to direct dialogue.

The consensus might not be fit for purpose, but something else needs to replace it. Something that alludes to common ground or the possibility of some kinds of limited cooperation – even if only in the cultural sphere or the economic one – might be sufficient. Taiwanese would accept nothing that seems to imply subservience or that opens the door to acknowledging China's claim on the island. But for any discussion to occur between two parties, however profound their disagreement, they first have to agree, in very general terms at least, on why they are engaging in dialogue and what the problem is that they are attempting to address. Anything that offered even a very basic foundation for Taiwan and China just to talk would be incredibly good news. But in 2024, the worst of all worlds prevails. Neither side talks to the other, nor do they have a theme they can talk within. This is very ominous.

Finally, Taiwan has to accept greater responsibility for its own protection. Its governments between 2000 and 2020 have been criticized for being complacent about funding for the armed forces and for civil defence. From a high of 5.1 per cent of GDP in 1988, military expenditure fell to 2.3 per cent of GDP in 2003. It then dropped to 1.7 per cent in 2019.[15] The rises in the defence budget since 2020 (in 2023, it was 2.6 per cent of GDP) are a sign that there is greater appreciation of the importance of the island's own defensive capabilities.[16] The brutal reality is that the more prepared, well-funded and modernized Taiwan's military, the more formidable the deterrent will be to China. The island will need to continue to increase this investment, but on the clear grounds of legitimate defence, even though it must avoid getting into an arms race with the mainland. It has to attend to its self-interest, and that means constant vigilance in maintaining at least some ability to defend itself, in order to dissuade China from thinking that any attack would be an easy undertaking.

Taiwanese have to accept that, if the crisis comes, and they wish to have a chance of preserving their freedoms and their territory, they will need to fight, no matter the cost. The people's willingness to engage in war is a crucial issue, but one that has not been tested for many decades. The government in Taipei needs to be clear with Taiwanese about this prospect. At the same time, it must avoid giving the impression it is preparing the island's population for a war that it desires, rather than for one it fears from others.

Hold the Fort

One of the many descriptions applied to Taiwan is that it is the world's largest aircraft carrier. It sits off the coast of China, like a huge potential military asset for any allies – a constant reminder to the PRC of its limitations and the restrictions placed on it by the outside world.

Taiwan's position, however, has never been more precarious. Uncertainty and danger swirl all around. There are many paradoxes in its current situation: its greatest source of strength – its commitment to its own identity and survival – is also a cause of its vulnerability. The more Taiwanese that Taiwan becomes, the more China grows restive and nervous. And while China regards reunification as its greatest strategic goal, it is the one issue above all others where a wrong step or a faulty move could destroy everything it has achieved in the last decades.

Today, there are no easy or immediate solutions to the

challenge of Taiwan. The current trajectories of Chinese and Taiwanese identity are incompatible; the aims of the mainland and those of most in Taiwan are diametrically opposed. Despite this, some in the outside world are playing an increasingly active, but sometimes unhelpful, role in dealing with this problem, lulled into a belief that the issue might be simpler to address than it is.

The policy framework of one China and strategic ambiguity is frayed and straining under immense pressure. And yet it still offers the only viable way to manage this issue – at least for now. Patience is paramount. The only solace is that at least Taiwan is not alone here. There are many other issues that cannot currently be solved, from the conflict between North and South Korea, to the impact of global warming, and the prevalence of inequality and poverty in human societies across the planet. That means a great deal of policy is simply about managing, and trying to avoid worst-case outcomes. In the case of Taiwan, those worst-case outcomes are truly cataclysmic. That should inspire a desire to manage this issue with the seriousness it deserves.

Strategic ambiguity, in particular, has started to fade from view in recent years. The assertive behaviour of China under Xi Jinping has coaxed players in the US and elsewhere to want to take a more active and committed position regarding Taiwan in order to counter it. While understandable, this is unwise. It either emboldens Taiwanese leaders to edge even closer to the red line of announcing Taiwan's independence, or it antagonizes and provokes China so that it might misread the signals one day and respond impetuously, and disastrously.

A restoration of the understanding of strategic ambiguity and why it is so useful and important is now essential. The rationale for this is simple: it is the best way to maintain the current status quo, preserve the peace, and so live to see another day, when a better option or even a solution might become clearer. That is the unglamorous task the world now needs to urgently engage in. Everyone is a stakeholder in the Taiwan issue. Everyone needs to do what they can to preserve at least some level of stability. There may come a time when the whole context, the geography, the world around us, changes, and our entire view of the situation is transformed. But, for today, strenuous defence of the stalemate is all that we can meaningfully do. Anything else is insanity.

Acknowledgements

I would like to record my thanks to the Taipei Representative Office in London for arranging a number of interviews and talks in preparation for this book. I am also grateful to HE Joseph Wu, and to Audrey Tang, Minister for Digital Affairs in the Taiwanese government, for allowing themselves to be interviewed. I am grateful for help, while in Taiwan in early January 2024, to Wu Tzu-hui in arranging access to the final rallies for the presidential campaign then being held, and to the Taiwan Semiconductor Manufacturing Company press office for their assistance in visiting the TSMC Museum of Innovation. I would also like to thank my doctoral student Sze Woon Miller for her help in some of the scenarios portrayed in the penultimate chapter. Research funding from King's College London has helped support my work on this book.

Over the years, I have accrued endless other debts in trying to understand Taiwanese politics and international relations. I am grateful for all the colleagues, friends and scholars who have helped me in gaining a better understanding. In particular, the late Bruce Jacobs, who was a veteran of Taiwan studies, and a first-hand witness to some of the key events that happened in the era of democratization.

Finally, I am grateful to Greg Clowes, who commissioned the book on behalf of Penguin, for his excellent stewardship and help in bringing it together. I am also grateful to Kit Shepherd for his careful work copy-editing the manuscript. As with every book, it has been a wonderful learning process, and one where I discovered that the issues I believed I knew well quickly transformed before me as I thought about them more.

Notes

Introduction

1 Amy Hawkins, 'Taiwan Foreign Minister Warns of Conflict with China in 2027', *Guardian*, 21 April 2023, https://www.theguardian. com/world/2023/apr/21/taiwan-foreign-minister-warns-of-conflict-with-china-in-2027.

1. Taiwan Life

1 Rupert Wingfield-Hayes, 'The Taiwan That China Wants is Vanishing', BBC News, 10 January 2024, https://www.bbc.co.uk/news/world-asia-67920287.
2 Christine Huang and Kelsey Jo Starr, 'Most People in Taiwan See Themselves as Primarily Taiwanese; Few Say They're Primarily Chinese', Pew Research Center, 16 January 2024, https://www. pewresearch.org/short-reads/2024/01/16/most-people-in-taiwan-see-themselves-as-primarily-taiwanese-few-say-theyre-primarily-chinese/.
3 'Taiwanese / Chinese Identity (1992/06~2023/12)', Election Study Center, National Chengchi University, https://esc.nccu.edu.tw/PageDoc/Detail?fid=7800&id=6961 (accessed 26 April 2024).
4 Jeffrey W. Hornung, 'Strong but Constrained Japan–Taiwan Ties', Brookings Institution, 13 March 2018, https://www.brookings. edu/articles/strong-but-constrained-japan-taiwan-ties/; 'Taiwan Welcomes 4 Millionth Visitor in 2023', Focus Taiwan, 13 September

2023, https://focustaiwan.tw/society/202309130009; Huang Tzu-ti, 'Taiwanese Tourists Biggest Foreign Spenders in Japan for Q2', *Taiwan News*, 23 July 2023, https://www.taiwannews.com.tw/news/4951559. In the latest available data, for the first nine months of 2023, the figure was 530,000 visitors from Japan to Taiwan; while, in the second quarter, 984,000 went from Taiwan to Japan.

5 'Taiwan', International Center for Not-for-Profit Law, https://www.icnl.org/resources/civic-freedom-monitor/taiwan (accessed 9 December 2023).

6 '2022 Report on International Religious Freedom', American Institute in Taiwan, 7 June 2023, https://www.ait.org.tw/2022-report-on-international-religious-freedom-taiwan/.

7 Worldometer, https://www.worldometers.info/coronavirus/country/taiwan/ (accessed 26 April 2024).

8 See 'Divorce within Five Years of Marriage at 10-Year High', *Taipei Times*, 25 July 2022, https://www.taipeitimes.com/News/taiwan/archives/2022/07/25/2003782387.

9 Jimmy Chuang, 'Dreaded Gangster Caught after Gunfight', *Taipei Times*, 14 July 2005, https://www.taipeitimes.com/News/front/archives/2005/07/14/2003263424.

10 Lily LaMattina, 'Indians in Taiwan Saddened by Online Racism', *Taiwan News*, 23 November 2023, https://www.taiwannews.com.tw/news/5045841.

11 'Statement by the Foreign Ministers of the G7 on the Launch of an Intercontinental Ballistic Missile by North Korea', Foreign, Commonwealth and Development Office, 19 December 2023, https://www.gov.uk/government/news/north-korea-missile-launch-statement-by-g7-foreign-ministers.

12 Eric Cheung, Will Ripley and Nectar Gan, 'Tensions High in the Waters off Taiwan Islands Visible from China's Shore. But for Locals, Life Goes On', CNN, 29 February 2024, https://edition.

cnn.com/2024/03/01/asia/taiwan-kinmen-life-goes-on-intl-hnk/index.html.

13 'The Most Dangerous Place on Earth', *The Economist*, 1 May 2021, https://www.economist.com/leaders/2021/05/01/the-most-dangerous-place-on-earth.

14 'China's Warplane Incursions into Taiwan Air Defence Zone Doubled in 2022', *Guardian*, 2 January 2023, https://www.theguardian.com/world/2023/jan/02/chinas-warplane-incursions-into-taiwan-air-defence-zone-doubled-in-2022.

15 Yimou Lee and Sarah Wu, 'China Satellite Launch Causes Pre-election Political Storm in Taiwan', Reuters, 10 January 2024, https://www.reuters.com/world/asia-pacific/taiwan-does-not-consider-china-satellite-launch-election-interference-2024-01-09/.

16 The Ministry of Defence subsequently admitted it had to change its messaging, and the text which had gone out was misleading.

17 Alice Fowle, 'Weather Tracker: Typhoon Koinu Causes Disruption in Taiwan', *Guardian*, 6 October 2023, https://www.theguardian.com/world/2023/oct/06/weather-tracker-typhoon-koinu-disruption-taiwan.

18 'Taiwan: Typhoon Haikui Makes Second Landfall', Deutsche Welle, 3 September 2023, https://www.dw.com/en/taiwan-typhoon-haikui-makes-second-landfall/a-66705629.

19 'Taipei Records Hottest Temperature in City's History', Focus Taiwan, 24 July 2020, https://focustaiwan.tw/society/202007240019.

20 'Combating Climate Change – Taiwan Can Help', Ministry of Foreign Affairs, Republic of China on Taiwan, 13 September 2018, https://en.mofa.gov.tw/News_Content.aspx?n=1575&s=34810.

21 'Taiwan Earthquake of 1999', Encyclopedia Britannica, 14 September 2023, https://www.britannica.com/event/Taiwan-earthquake-of-1999.

2. How It Started, How It's Going: Taiwan's History

1 The whole dramatic saga is expertly told in Adam Brookes, *Fragile Cargo: The World War II Race to Save the Treasures of China's Forbidden City*, Simon and Schuster, New York and London, 2023.

2 Rubinstein, 29–37.

3 Rubinstein, 85.

4 Manthorpe, 34.

5 Rubinstein, 86.

6 Su Beng, 14.

7 Keliher, 189.

8 Kerr, 91.

9 Yang, 7.

10 Yang, 88.

11 'Mutual Defense Treaty between the United States and the Republic of China', 2 December 1954, Article II, available at https://avalon.law.yale.edu/20th_century/chin001.asp.

12 Taylor, 572.

13 Neil H. Jacoby, 'An Evaluation of U.S. Economic Aid to Free China. 1951–1965', Bureau for the Far East Agency for International Development, Washington DC, January 1966, p. i, https://pdf.usaid.gov/pdf_docs/PNAAK054.pdf.

14 Kelly Olds, 'The Economic History of Taiwan', Economic History Association, 16 March 2008, https://eh.net/encyclopedia/the-economic-history-of-taiwan/.

15 Rigger, 1999, 140–42.

3. Becoming Taiwanese: Democracy in Action

1 Lee, 181.

2 Lee, 51.

3 See Su Chi, 52–85.

4 Su Chi.

5 Su Chi, 290.

6 'President Tsai Issues Statement Regarding the Situation in Hong Kong', Office of the President, Republic of China ('Taiwan'), 13 June 2023, https://english.president.gov.tw/News/5755.

7 Brian Hiao, 'Han Kuo-yu Causes Controversy after Recent String of Gaffes', New Bloom, 29 October 2019, https://newbloommag.net/2019/10/29/han-kuo-yu-gaffes/.

8 Amber Wang and Sean Chang, 'Taiwan President Tsai Ing-wen Quits Party Leadership after Polls Setback', Hong Kong Free Press, 24 November 2018, https://hongkongfp.com/2018/11/24/just-tai wan-president-tsai-ing-wen-quits-party-leadership-polls-setback/.

9 'Taiwan Independence vs. Unification with the Mainland (1994/12~2023/12)', Election Study Center, National Chengchi University, 22 February 2024, https://esc.nccu.edu.tw/Page-Doc/Detail?fid=7801&id=6963.

10 'Public Perception That Chinese Authorities are Unfriendly to Taiwan Reaches New High; Over 90% Surveyed Oppose the CCP's "One Country, Two Systems" and Its Suppression of Taiwan through Military and Diplomatic Means', Mainland Affairs Council, Taiwan, 26 March 2020, https://www.mac.gov.tw/en/News_Content.aspx?n=A921DFB2651FF92F&sms=3783 8322A6DA5E79&s=4C12F840F128DD2E.

11 Tim McDonald, 'China and Taiwan Face Off in Pineapple War', BBC News, 19 March 2021, https://www.bbc.co.uk/news/business-56353963.

12 Meng Chih-cheng, 'Support for Independence Grows,' *Taipei Times*, 16 June 2023, https://www.taipeitimes.com/News/editor ials/archives/2023/06/16/2003801614.

13 David Sacks, 'Taiwan Announced a Record Defense Budget: But is It Enough to Deter China?', Council on Foreign Relations, 30 August 2023, https://www.cfr.org/blog/taiwan-announced-record-defense-budget-it-enough-deter-china.

14 Matt Yu and Ko Lin, 'Conscripts Starting 1-Year Military Service Report to Boot Camps', Focus Taiwan, 25 January 2024, https://focustaiwan.tw/politics/202401250022.

15 Fell, 2018, 99.

16 Bush, 2005, 283.

17 Clement Tan, ' "Taiwan is China's Taiwan": Beijing Says Taiwan's Ruling Party is Not Representative of Popular Opinion', CNBC, 13 January 2024, https://www.cnbc.com/2024/01/13/china-reacts-to-pivotal-taiwan-presidential-election.html.

4. *The Role of Taiwan's Economy and the Superconductors That Power Information Technology*

1   'What is a Semiconductor?', Semiconductor Industry Association, https://www.semiconductors.org/semiconductors-101/what-is-a-semiconductor/ (accessed 4 May 2024).

2   Sean Ashcroft, 'What Caused the Semiconductor Shortage?', Supply Chain, 11 January 2023, https://supplychaindigital.com/top10/timeline-causes-of-the-global-semiconductor-shortage.

3   'The World's Largest Economies', WorldData.info, February 2024, https://www.worlddata.info/largest-economies.php.

4   Matthew Mazzetta, 'Taiwan the 14th Richest Country in the World: Global Finance', Focus Taiwan, 25 December 2023, https://focustai wan.tw/business/202312250013.

5 Kelly Olds, 'The Economic History of Taiwan', Economic History Association, 16 March 2008, https://eh.net/encyclopedia/the-economic-history-of-taiwan/.

6 Breznitz, 7.

7 Berger and Lester, 3–4.

8 Breznitz, 10.

9 Berger and Lester, 6.

10 Breznitz, 104.

11 'Oral History Interview: Morris Chang', SEMI, 24 August 2007, https://www.semi.org/en/Oral-History-Interview-Morris-Chang. Much of the following account of Chang's life is based on this interview.

12 'Market Capitalization of TSMC (TSM)', Companies Market Cap, https://companiesmarketcap.com/tsmc/marketcap/ (accessed 4 May 2024).

13 Paul Mozur and John Liu, 'The Chip Titan Whose Life's Work is at the Center of a Tech Cold War', *New York Times*, 4 August 2023, https://www.nytimes.com/2023/08/04/technology/the-chip-titan-whose-lifes-work-is-at-the-center-of-a-tech-cold-war.html.

14 See Miller, 228.

15 Evelyn Cheng, 'China Needs Taiwan's Biggest Chipmaker – More Than the Other Way Around', CNBC, 16 August 2022, https://www.cnbc.com/2022/08/17/china-needs-taiwans-biggest-chipmaker-more-than-the-other-way-around.html.

16 Frederik Kelter, 'The Battle over Semiconductors is Endangering Taiwan', *Foreign Policy*, 9 November 2022, https://foreignpolicy.com/2022/11/09/tsmc-taiwan-battle-semiconductors-water-resource-scarcity/.

17 Paul Mozur and John Liu, 'The Chip Titan Whose Life's Work is at the Center of a Tech Cold War', *New York Times*, 4 August 2023, https://www.nytimes.com/2023/08/04/technology/the-chip-titan-whose-lifes-work-is-at-the-center-of-a-tech-cold-war.html.

18 Rupert Wingfield-Hayes, 'Terry Gou: The Taiwan iPhone Billionaire Who Wants to be President', BBC News, 28 August 2023, https://www.bbc.co.uk/news/world-asia-66639012.

19 Liu Xiaobo, *No Enemies, No Hatred: Selected Essays and Poems*, ed. Perry Link, Tienchi Martin-Lioa and Liu Xia, Belknap Press, Cambridge, MA, 2012, 210.

20 Brian Merchant, 'Life and Death in Apple's Forbidden City', *Guardian*, 18 June 2017, https://www.theguardian.com/technol ogy/2017/jun/18/foxconn-life-death-forbidden-city-longhua-sui cide-apple-iphone-brian-merchant-one-device-extract.

21 David Barboza, 'Electronics Maker Promises Review after Suicides', *New York Times*, 26 May 2010, https://www.nytimes. com/2010/05/27/technology/27suicide.html.

22 See Lee Chun-yi, 'From Being Privileged to Being Localized? Taiwanese Businessmen in China', in Chu Kuei-fen, Dafydd Fell and Ping Lin (eds.), *Migration to and from Taiwan*, Routledge, London and New York, 2014, 57–72.

23 'Foxconn Founder Terry Gou Announces Taiwan Presidential Bid', France 24, 28 August 2023, https://www.france24.com/en/ asia-pacific/20230828-foxconn-founder-terry-gou-announces-tai wan-presidential-bid.

24 Dennis L. C. Weng and Jared Jeter, 'Commentary: Foxconn Founder Terry Gou's Presidential Candidacy May Shift Taiwan's Political Landscape', CNA, 15 November 2023, https://www.chan nelnewsasia.com/commentary/terry-gou-taiwan-presidential-election-2024-foxconn-one-china-3919271.

25 Zhang Wensheng, 'What Will Terry Gou's Candidacy Bring to Taiwan', *Global Times*, 28 August 2023, https://www.globaltimes. cn/page/202308/1297135.shtml.

26 Yimou Lee and Ben Blanchard, 'Terry Gou Withdraws from Taiwan President Race, Bringing Relief to Foxconn', Reuters, 24 November 2023, https://www.reuters.com/world/asia-pacific/

foxconn-founder-terry-gou-withdraws-race-be-taiwan-president-2023-11-24/.

27 Wilson Center statistic, quoted in Lee Ying Shan, 'China De-linking Talk is Overdone and It's Still Key to the Global Economy, Asian Development Bank Says', CNBC, 25 February 2024, https://www. cnbc.com/2024/02/26/china-still-top-trading-partner-for-many-countries-says-adb.html#:~:text=However%2C%20the%20econo mic%20powerhouse%20remains,U.S.%20think%20tank%20Wilson %20Center.

28 Nur Shahadah Jamil, 'Taiwan's New Southbound Policy in Southeast Asia and the "China Factor": Deepening Regional Integration Amid New Reality', *Asian Affairs*, vol. 54, no. 2, June 2023, 264.

29 Jamil, 275.

30 Sana Hashmi, 'Situating India in Taiwan's New Southbound Policy', *Asian Affairs*, vol. 54, no. 2, June 2023, 314–15.

31 Interview with the author, 26 December 2023.

32 Nick Aspinwall, 'Taiwan's Human Rights Miracle Does Not Extend to Its Southeast Asian Foreign Workers', *The Diplomat*, 10 October 2019, https://thediplomat.com/2019/10/taiwans-human-rights-miracle-does-not-extend-to-its-southeast-asian-foreign-workers/.

33 Tsao Yao-chun, 'Taiwan the Happiest in East Asia', *Taipei Times*, 28 March 2021, https://www.taipeitimes.com/News/editorials/archives/2021/03/28/2003754618.

34 Chien-Hua Wan and Betty Hou, 'Taiwan Cuts 2023 Growth Outlook to Lowest since Financial Crisis', Bloomberg, 28 November 2023, https://www.bloomberg.com/news/articles/2023-11-28/taiwan-cuts-2023-growth-outlook-to-lowest-since-financial-crisis.

35 'Taiwan's Working Hours 6th Longest among 39 Economies in 2022: MOL', Focus Taiwan, 7 October 2023, https://focustaiwan.tw/business/202310070017.

36 'Cost of Living – Taiwanese Workers Unhappy with Their Largely Stagnant Salaries: Survey', Focus Taiwan, 6 September 2023, https://focustaiwan.tw/business/202309060014.

37 Pan Tzu-yu and France Huang, 'Cost of Living – CPI Growth in 2023 Hits 2nd Highest Level in 15 Years', Focus Taiwan, 5 January 2024, https://focustaiwan.tw/business/202401050017.

5. China's Relations with Taiwan: Friends or Enemies?

1 Charlie Campbell, 'Leaders of China and Taiwan Meet for the First Time', *Time*, 7 November 2015, https://time.com/4103732/china-taiwan-xi-jinping-ma-ying-jeou/.

2 Min-Hua Chiang, 'Why China's Solo Tourist Ban is Not a Big Deal for Taiwan', Taiwan Insight, 16 September 2019, https://taiwaninsight.org/2019/09/16/why-chinas-solo-tourist-ban-is-not-a-big-deal-for-taiwan/.

3 Ralph Jennings, 'Taiwanese Workers Leaving Mainland China over Covid-19, Political Tensions, Factory Departures', *South China Morning Post*, 12 April 2023, https://www.scmp.com/economy/global-economy/article/3216799/taiwanese-workers-leaving-mainland-china-over-covid-19-political-tensions-factory-departures.

4 Michelle Zhang, 'What Life is Like as a Taiwanese Living in Mainland China', Worldcrunch, 13 October 2022, https://worldcrunch.com/culture-society/taiwanese-in-mainland-china.

5 Kat Devlin and Christine Huang, 'In Taiwan, Views of Mainland China Mostly Negative', Pew Research Center, 12 May 2020, https://www.pewresearch.org/global/2020/05/12/in-taiwan-views-of-mainland-china-mostly-negative/.

6 Chung Li-hua and Jonathan Chin, 'Poll Shows 48.9% Support Independence', *Taipei Times*, 2 September 2023, https://www.taipeitimes.com/News/taiwan/archives/2023/09/02/2003805648#:

~:text=A%20poll%20released%20by%20the,percent%20support %20unification%20with%20China.

7 Yu Sen-lun, ' "Hu's Talking" Provides an Insider's View of Jason Hu', *Taipei Times*, 27 February 2000, https://www.taipeitimes. com/News/feat/archives/2000/02/27/0000025843.

8 'Ye Jianying on Taiwan's Return to Motherland and Peaceful Reunification', 30 September 1981, China.org, http://www.china. org.cn/english/7945.htm (accessed 7 May 2024).

9 'Jan 30,1995: President Jiang Zemin Puts Forward Eight Propositions on Development of Relations between Two Sides of Taiwan Straits', *China Daily*, 30 January 2011, https://www.chinadaily.com.cn/ china/19thcpcnationalcongress/2011-01/30/content_29715090.htm.

10 'President Hu Sets Forth Guidelines on Taiwan', Embassy of the People's Republic of China in the Republic of the Philippines, 5 March 2005, http://ph.china-embassy.gov.cn/eng/zt/twwt/ 200503/t20050305_1334812.htm.

11 Chris Buckley and Chris Horton, 'Xi Jinping Warns Taiwan That Unification is the Goal and Force is an Option', *New York Times*, 1 January 2019, https://www.nytimes.com/2019/01/01/world/asia/ xi-jinping-taiwan-china.html.

12 The Taiwan Affairs Office of the State Council and the State Council Information Office, 'The Taiwan Question and China's Reunification in the New Era', August 2022, Preamble and Section III.1, available at https://english.www.gov.cn/archive/whitepa per/202208/10/content_WS62f34f46c6d02e533532f0ac.html.

13 Evelyn Cheng, 'Taiwan's Trade with China is Far Bigger than Its Trade with the U.S.', CNBC, https://www.cnbc.com/2022/ 08/05/taiwans-trade-with-china-is-far-bigger-than-its-trade-with- the-us.html.

14 'Cross-strait Relations: Fact Focus', Government Portal of the Republic of China, https://www.taiwan.gov.tw/content_6.php (accessed 7 May 2024).

15 Lee, 121.

16 'Interview of Taiwan President Lee Teng-hui with Deutsche Welle Radio', 9 July 1999, available at New Taiwan, https://www.taiwandc.org/nws-9926.htm.

17 'President Chen Shui-bian's New Year's Day Message and the Development of Cross-strait Relations', 18 January 2006, Mainland Affairs Council, Taiwan, General Policy Archives (1994–2008), https://www.mac.gov.tw/en/News_Content.aspx?n=8A319E37A32E01EA&sms=2413CFE1BCE87E0E&s=3E550941C8EDA065.

18 Chris Buckley and Ralph Jennings, 'China Slams Independence Talk from Taiwan', Reuters, 9 August 2007, https://www.reuters.com/article/idUSTP314144/.

19 'Ma Ying-jeou, "Inaugural Address," May 20, 2008', USC US-China Institute, https://china.usc.edu/ma-ying-jeou-%E2%80%9Cinaugural-address%E2%80%9D-may-20-2008.

20 See Stuart Lau, 'China Bombards Taiwan with Fake News Ahead of Election', *Politico*, 10 January 2024, https://www.politico.eu/article/china-bombards-taiwan-with-fake-news-ahead-of-election/.

21 'Xi Jinping Meets with Taiwan Delegation Led by Lien Chan', Xinhua, 13 July 2018, http://www.xinhuanet.com/english/2018-07/13/c_137322460.htm.

22 'Funeral for Uncle of China's First Lady Held in Chiayi; KMT Officials Attend', *Taipei Times*, 24 November 2016, https://www.taipeitimes.com/News/taiwan/archives/2016/11/24/2003659894.

23 Katsuji Nakazawa, 'Analysis: For 17 years, Xi Closely Watched Taiwan-governed Islets', Nikkei Asia, 6 July 2023, https://asia.nikkei.com/Editor-s-Picks/China-up-close/Analysis-For-17-years-Xi-closely-watched-Taiwan-governed-islets.

24 Wedeman.

25 See Brown, 74–5.

26 'Xi Jinping, First Speech as General Secretary, Nov. 15, 2012', USC US-China Institute, https://china.usc.edu/xi-jinping-first-speech-general-secretary-nov-15-2012.

27 Tom Phillips, 'China's Xi Jinping Denies House of Cards Power Struggle but Attacks "Conspirators"', *Guardian*, 4 May 2016, https://www.theguardian.com/world/2016/may/04/china-xi-jinping-house-of-cards-attacks-conspirators.

28 Chen Yu-fu and William Hetherington, 'Visitors to China Being Interrogated, Detained', *Taipei Times*, 5 December 2023, https://www.taipeitimes.com/News/taiwan/archives/2023/12/05/2003810164.

29 Ben Doherty et al., 'Taiwan Official in Hospital after Alleged "Violent Attack" by Chinese Diplomats in Fiji', *Guardian*, 19 October 2020, https://www.theguardian.com/world/2020/oct/19/taiwan-official-in-hospital-after-alleged-violent-attack-by-chinese-diplomats-in-fiji.

30 Elizabeth Redden, 'Censorship at China Studies Meeting', Inside Higher Ed, 5 August 2014, https://www.insidehighered.com/news/2014/08/06/accounts-confucius-institute-ordered-censorship-chinese-studies-conference.

31 'Full Text of President Xi Jinping's 2024 New Year Message', Ministry of Foreign Affairs for the People's Republic of China, 31 December 2023, https://www.mfa.gov.cn/eng/zxxx_662805/202312/t20231231_11215608.html#:~:text=China%20will%20surely%20be%20reunified,better%20life%20for%20the%20people.

32 Helen Davidson and Julian Borger, 'China Could Mount Full-Scale Invasion by 2025, Taiwan Defence Minister Says', *Guardian*, 6 October 2021, https://www.theguardian.com/world/2021/oct/06/biden-says-he-and-chinas-xi-have-agreed-to-abide-by-taiwan-agreement.

33 Doina Chiacu, 'U.S. Defense Secretary Sees No Imminent Invasion of Taiwan by China', Reuters, 2 October 2022, https://

www.reuters.com/world/asia-pacific/us-defense-secretary-sees-no-imminent-invasion-taiwan-by-china-2022-10-02/#:~:text=%22I%20don%E2%80%99t%20see%20an,number%20has%20increased%20over%20time.

34 Thompson Chau, 'China Doubles Down on Taiwan Threats as Election Nears', Nikkei Asia, 10 November 2023, https://asia.nikkei.com/Politics/Taiwan-elections/China-doubles-down-on-Taiwan-threats-as-election-nears.

35 Mary Bruce, Luke Barr and Justin Fishel, 'Xi Told Biden at Summit That China Plans to Reunify with Taiwan', ABC News, 20 December 2023, https://abcnews.go.com/International/xi-warns-biden-china-plans-back-taiwan/story?id=105815520.

36 Helen Davidson, 'Taiwan President Says China Has Too Many Problems to Invade', *Guardian*, 30 November 2023, https://www.theguardian.com/world/2023/nov/30/taiwan-president-tsai-ing-wen-china-problems-invade-xi-jinping.

6. *Taiwan and the US: Allies Indeed?*

1 Alys Davies, 'Taiwan Tensions: China Condemns "Manic" Visit as Pelosi Continues Tour', BBC News, 4 August 2022, https://www.bbc.co.uk/news/world-asia-62419855.

2 David Smith, 'Pelosi's "Reckless" Taiwan Visit Deepens US–China Rupture – Why Did She Go?', *Guardian*, 7 August 2022, https://www.theguardian.com/us-news/2022/aug/07/nancy-pelosi-taiwan-china-visit-military.

3 Jenny Leonard and Billy House, 'Pelosi's Taiwan Trip Left a Fuming White House Scrambling for a Plan', Bloomberg, 3 August 2022, https://www.bloomberg.com/news/articles/2022-08-03/pelosi-s-taiwan-trip-left-white-house-scrambling-for-a-plan.

4 Nancy Pelosi, 'Why I'm Leading a Congressional Delegation to Taiwan', *Washington Post*, 2 August 2022, https://www.washington post.com/opinions/2022/08/02/nancy-pelosi-taiwan-visit-op-ed/.

5 Interview with the author, 4 December 2023.

6 Declassified top secret memorandum, conversation between Henry Kissinger and Chou Enlai, 6 August 1971, 4, 16, 19, The National Security Archive, https://nsarchive2.gwu.edu/NSAEBB /NSAEBB66/ch-35.pdf.

7 Dave Makichuk, 'Taiwan Can Wait 100 Years, Mao Told Nixon', China Factor, 22 November 2021, https://chinafactor.news/2021/ 11/22/taiwan-can-wait-100-years-mao-told-nixon/.

8 'Joint Communique between the United States and China', 27 February 1972, available at https://digitalarchive.wilsoncenter. org/document/joint-communique-between-united-states-and-china.

9 Henry Kamm, 'Taiwanese Attack U.S. Motorcade as Officials Arrive for Negotiations', *New York Times*, 28 December 1978, https:// www.nytimes.com/1978/12/28/archives/taiwanese-attack-us-motorcade-as-officials-arrive-for-negotiations.html.

10 'U.S.–PRC Joint Communique (1979)', 15 December 1978, available at https://www.ait.org.tw/u-s-prc-joint-communique-1979/ #:~:text=(The%20communique%20was%20released%20on,as% 20of%20January%201%2C%201979.

11 'H.R. 2479, 96th Congress (1979–1980): Taiwan Relations Act', 10 April 1979, available at https://www.congress.gov/bill/96th-con gress/house-bill/2479/text.

12 U.S.–PRC Joint Communique (1982)', 17 August 1982, available at https://www.ait.org.tw/u-s-prc-joint-communique-1982/.

13 Kelly Wallace, 'Bush Pledges Whatever It Takes to Defend Taiwan', CNN, 25 April 2001, https://edition.cnn.com/2001/ ALLPOLITICS/04/24/bush.taiwan.abc/index.html.

14 Frank Ching, 'Has President Chen Learned His Lesson?', *Japan Times*, 15 May 2004, https://www.japantimes.co.jp/opinion/2004/05/15/commentary/has-president-chen-learned-his-lesson/. Hickey, 100.

15 'Donald Trump Calls Chinese President Xi Jinping "Brilliant Man" Who Rules with "Iron Fist"', *Economic Times*, 20 July 2023, https://economictimes.indiatimes.com/news/international/us/ex-u-s-president-donald-trump-praises-chinese-president-xi-jinping/articleshow/101992752.cms; David Shepardson, 'Trump Praises Chinese President Extending Tenure "for Life"', Reuters, 4 March 2018, https://www.reuters.com/article/idUSKCN1GG03P/; Ben Westcott and Nikki Cavarjal, 'US President Trump Says He Called Xi Jinping the "King" of China", CNN, 2 April 2019, https://edition.cnn.com/2019/04/02/politics/trump-xi-king-of-china-intl/index.html.

16 Ben Blanchard, 'U.S. Should Recognise Taiwan, Former Top Diplomat Pompeo Says', Reuters, 4 March 2022, https://www.reuters.com/world/asia-pacific/us-should-recognise-taiwan-former-top-diplomat-pompeo-says-2022-03-04/#:~:text=%22While%20the%20United%20States%20should,as%20secondary%2C%22%20Pompeo%20said.

17 Ben Blanchard, 'U.S. Former Top Diplomat Pompeo Arrives in Taiwan, Calls It "Great Nation"', Reuters, 2 March 2022, https://www.reuters.com/world/us-former-top-diplomat-pompeo-arrives-taiwan-calls-it-great-nation-2022-03-02/#:~:text=TAIPEI%2C%20March%202%20(Reuters),sensitive%20red%20line%20for%20Beijing.

18 Li Yang, 'Pompeo Fishing for Personal Gains with Taiwan Visit', *China Daily*, 30 September 2022, https://global.chinadaily.com.cn/a/202209/30/WS63362c26a310fd2b29e7a8d0.html.

19 Helen Davidson, 'Liz Truss in Taiwan Calls for "Economic Nato" to Challenge China', *Guardian*, 17 May 2023, https://www.the

guardian.com/world/2023/may/17/liz-truss-in-taiwan-calls-for-economic-nato-to-challenge-china.

20 Becky Morton, 'Liz Truss Taiwan Trip Sparks Row with Senior Tory MP', BBC News, 11 May 2023, https://www.bbc.co.uk/news/uk-politics-65556086.

21 Meaghan Tobin and Ellen Nakashima, 'Taiwan's President to Stop in U.S., Raising Prospect of Friction with China', *Washington Post*, 21 March 2023, https://www.washingtonpost.com/world/2023/03/21/taiwan-tsai-china-united-states/.

22 Interview with the author, 4 December 2023.

7. *What If a Cross-strait War Started?*

1 David Brunnstrom, 'U.S. Position on Taiwan Unchanged Despite Biden Comment – Official', Reuters, 20 August 2021, https://www.reuters.com/world/asia-pacific/us-position-taiwan-unchanged-despite-biden-comment-official-2021-08-19/.

2 Trevor Hunnicutt, 'Biden Says United States Would Come to Taiwan's Defense', Reuters, 22 October 2021, https://www.reuters.com/world/asia-pacific/biden-says-united-states-would-come-taiwans-defense-2021-10-22/#:~:text=BALTIMORE%2C%20Oct%2021%20(Reuters),in%20policy%20towards%20the%20island.

3 'Biden Tells 60 Minutes U.S. Troops Would Defend Taiwan, but White House Says This is Not Official U.S. Policy', CBS News, 18 September 2022, https://www.cbsnews.com/news/president-joe-biden-taiwan-60-minutes-2022-09-18/.

4 David Brunnstrom and Trevor Hunnicutt, 'Biden Says U.S. Forces Would Defend Taiwan in the Event of a Chinese Invasion', Reuters, 19 September 2022, https://www.reuters.com/world/biden-says-us-forces-would-defend-taiwan-event-chinese-invasion-2022-09-18/.

5 Bush, 2005, 1–2.

6 'Full Text of President Xi Jinping's 2024 New Year Message', Ministry of Foreign Affairs for the People's Republic of China, 31 December 2023, https://www.mfa.gov.cn/eng/zxxx_662805/202312/t20231231_11215608.html#:~:text=China%20will%20surely%20be%20reunified,better%20life%20for%20the%20people.

7 Amrita Jash, 'At the 2024 "Two Sessions" in Beijing, China Talks Tough on Taiwan', Global Taiwan Institute, 20 March 2024, https://globaltaiwan.org/2024/03/at-the-2024-two-sessions-in-beijing-china-talks-tough-on-taiwan/.

8 Srishti Singh Sisodia, 'US Senator Refers to Taiwan as "Country", Vows Support to Help It Become an "Independent Nation"', WION, 26 August 2022, https://www.wionews.com/world/us-senator-refers-to-taiwan-as-country-vows-to-support-it-to-become-independent-nation-510358.

9 Tom Tiffany, website, 25 January 2023, https://tiffany.house.gov/media/editorials-letters-and-articles/exclusive-rep-tiffany-introduces-resolution-calling-us.

10 Liu Tzu-hsuan, 'US Lawmaker Hopes for Independence', *Taipei Times*, 5 July 2023, https://www.taipeitimes.com/News/front/archives/2023/07/05/2003802688.

11 Wuthnow et al. (eds.), 6.

12 Wuthnow et al. (eds.), 8.

13 Clausewitz, 117.

14 Wuthnow et al. (eds.), 9.

15 Charlie Vest, Agatha Kratz and Reva Goujon, 'The Global Economic Disruptions from a Taiwan Conflict', Rhodium Group, 14 December 2022, https://rhg.com/research/taiwan-economic-disruptions/.

16 Richard Engel et al., 'Why War with China over Taiwan Could Ruin the Global Economy', NBC News, 29 June 2023, https://www.nbcnews.com/news/world/taiwan-war-china-us-ruin-global-economy-semiconductors-chips-rcna91321.

8. Thinking Through the Future: The Taiwan Challenge in the Twenty-first Century

1 Quoted in Robin Niblett, *The New Cold War: How the Contest Between the US and China Will Shape Our Century*, Atlantic Books, London, 2024, 3.

2 Remarks carried in Chinese in the *China Times*, 8 March 2024, https://www.chinatimes.com/newspapers/20240308000417-2601 18?chdtv=.

3 See, for example, Mark Scott, 'Beijing Increases Military Pressure on Taiwan Ahead of US-China Talks', *Politico*, 27 January 2024, https://www.politico.eu/article/china-taiwan-military-pressure-united-states/; Phil Stewart and Idrees Ali, 'How the US is Preparing for a Chinese Invasion of Taiwan', Reuters, 31 January 2024, https://www.reuters.com/world/china/logistics-war-how-washington-is-preparing-chinese-invasion-taiwan-2024-01-31/; Michael Beckley and Hal Brands, 'How Primed for War is China?', *Foreign Policy*, 4 February 2024, https://foreignpolicy.com/2024/02/04/china-war-military-taiwan-us-asia-xi-escalation-crisis/; Tiffany Tsoi, Tracy Alloway and Joe Weisenthal, 'Here's What Could Happen If There's a War over Taiwan', Bloomberg, 16 January 2024, https://www.bloomberg.com/news/articles/2024-01-16/here-s-what-could-happen-if-there-s-a-war-over-taiwan.

4 Oriana Skylar Mastro, 'This is What America is Getting Wrong about China and Taiwan', *New York Times*, 16 October 2023, https://www.nytimes.com/2023/10/16/opinion/china-us-taiwan-war.html.

5 Robert A. Manning, 'Would Anyone "Win" a Taiwan Conflict?', Stimson, 9 January 2024, https://www.stimson.org/2024/us-china-taiwan-conflict-global-economy/.

6 Kiyoshi Takenaka, 'Abe Sees World War One Echoes in Japan-China Tensions', Reuters, 23 January 2014, https://www.reuters.

com/article/us-japan-china/abe-sees-world-war-one-echoes-in-japan-china-tensions-idUSBREA0M08G20140123/.

7 Scott Moore, 'The United States of China', *New York Times*, 11 March 2014, https://www.nytimes.com/2014/03/12/opinion/the-united-states-of-china.html.

8 Hugh White, 'The Harsh Reality That Taiwan Faces', *Straits Times*, 19 January 2016, https://www.straitstimes.com/opinion/the-harsh-reality-that-taiwan-faces.

9 One such critique is Peter Jennings's blog post on the Australian Strategic Policy Institute website, 'Too Soon to be Waving the White Flag on China', The Strategist, 24 November 2021, https://www.aspistrategist.org.au/too-soon-to-be-waving-the-white-flag-on-china/.

10 'Preventing War in the Taiwan Strait', International Crisis Group, 27 October 2023, https://www.crisisgroup.org/asia/north-east-asia/taiwan-strait-china/333-preventing-war-taiwan-strait.

11 Richard Bush, Bonnie Glaser and Ryan Hass, 'Don't Help China by Hyping Risk of War over Taiwan', NPR, 8 April 2021, https://www.npr.org/2021/04/08/984524521/opinion-dont-help-china-by-hyping-risk-of-war-over-taiwan.

12 Aiden Powers-Riggs, 'Taipei Fears Washington is Weakening Its Silicon Shield', *Foreign Policy*, 17 February 2023, https://foreign-policy.com/2023/02/17/united-states-taiwan-china-semiconductors-silicon-shield-chips-act-biden/.

13 See Ge.

14 Matt Pottinger and Mike Gallagher, 'No Substitute for Victory: America's Competition with China Must be Won, Not Managed', *Foreign Affairs*, May–June 2024, https://www.foreignaffairs.com/united-states/no-substitute-victory-pottinger-gallagher.

15 'Military Expenditure by Country as Percentage of Gross Domestic Product, 1988–2019', Stockholm International Peace Research

Institute, 2020, https://www.sipri.org/sites/default/files/Data%20for%20all%20countries%20from%201988%E2%80%932019%20as%20a%20share%20of%20GDP.pdf.

16 David Sacks, 'Taiwan Announced a Record Defense Budget: But is It Enough to Deter China?', Council on Foreign Relations, 30 August 2023, https://www.cfr.org/blog/taiwan-announced-record-defense-budget-it-enough-deter-china.

Select Bibliography

Ash, Robert, John W. Garver and Penelope B. Prime. *Taiwan's Democracy: Economic and Political Challenges*. Routledge, London and New York. 2011.

Barmé, Geremie, and John Minford (eds.). *Seeds of Fire: Chinese Voices of Conscience*. Bloodaxe Books, Newcastle upon Tyne. 1989.

Berger, Suzanne, and Richard K. Lester (eds.). *Global Taiwan: Building Competitive Strengths in a New International Economy*. M. E. Sharpe, Armonk, NY, and London. 2005.

Breznitz, Dan. *Innovation and the State: Political Choice and Strategies for Growth in Israel, Taiwan, and Ireland*. Yale University Press, New Haven, CT, and London. 2007.

Brown, Kerry. *Xi: A Study of Power*. Ikon Books, London. 2022.

Brown, Kerry, and Kalley Wu Tzu-hui. *The Trouble with Taiwan: History, the United States and a Rising China*. Zed Books, London. 2019.

Bush, Richard C. *Untying the Knot: Making Peace in the Taiwan Strait*. Brookings Institution Press, Washington DC. 2005.

Bush, Richard C. *Uncharted Strait: The Future of China–Taiwan Relations*. Brookings Institution Press, Washington DC. 2013.

Clausewitz, Carl von. *On War*. Edited and translated by Michael Howard and Peter Paret. Everyman, London. 1993.

Copper, John F. *Consolidating Taiwan's Democracy*. University Press of America, Lanham, MD. 2005.

Fell, Dafydd. *Party Politics in Taiwan: Party Change and the Democratic Evolution of Taiwan, 1991–2004*. Routledge, London and New York. 2005.

Fell, Dafydd. *Government and Politics in Taiwan*. Second edition. Routledge, London and New York. 2018.

Ge, Zhaoguang. *What is China? Territory, Ethnicity, Culture and History*. Translated by Michael Gibbs Hill. Belknap Press, Cambridge, MA. 2018.

Gilley, Bruce, and Larry Diamond. *Political Change in China: Comparisons with Taiwan*. Lynne Rienner Publishers, Boulder, CO, and London. 2008.

Guilloux, Alain. *Taiwan, Humanitarianism and Global Governance*. Routledge, London and New York. 2009.

Harrell, Stevan, and Huang Chün-chieh (eds.). *Cultural Change in Postwar Taiwan*. 1994. Reprinted Routledge, London and New York. 2019.

Hickey, Dennis Van Vranken. *Foreign Policy Making in Taiwan: From Principle to Pragmatism*. Routledge, London and New York. 2007.

Keliher, Macabe. *Out of China, or, Yu Yonghe's Tales of Formosa*. SMC Publishing, Taipei. 2003.

Kerr, George H. *Formosa Betrayed*. 1965. Reprinted Taiwan Publishing Co., Taipei, 1997.

Lee Teng-hui. *The Road to Democracy: Taiwan's Pursuit of Identity*. PHP Institute, Tokyo. 1999.

Liang, Qichao. *Thoughts from the Ice-drinker's Studio: Essays on China and the World*. Edited and translated by Peter Zarrow. Penguin Books, London. 2023.

Manthorpe, Jonathan. *Forbidden Nation: A History of Taiwan*. St Martin's Griffin, New York. 2009.

Mattlin, Mikael. *Politicized Society: Taiwan's Struggle with Its One-party Past*. Revised edition. Norwegian Institute of Asian Studies Press, Oslo. 2018.

Meyer, Mahlon. *Remembering China from Taiwan: Divided Families and Bittersweet Reunions after the Chinese Civil War*. Hong Kong University Press, Hong Kong. 2012.

Miller, Andrew. *Chip War: The Fight for the World's Most Critical Technology*. Scribner, New York. 2022.

Pai Hsien-yung. *Taipei People*. Chinese University Press, Hong Kong. 2000.

Peng, Ming-min. *A Taste of Freedom: Memoirs of a Taiwanese Independence Leader*. 1972–98. Reprinted Camphor Press, Manchester. 2019.

Rigger, Shelley. *Politics in Taiwan: Voting for Democracy*. Routledge, London and New York. 1999.

Rigger, Shelley. *Why Taiwan Matters: Small Island, Global Powerhouse*. Updated edition. Rowman and Littlefield, Lanham, MD. 2011.

Roy, Denny. *Taiwan: A Political History*. Cornell University Press, Ithaca, NY, and London. 2003.

Rubinstein, Murray A. (ed.). *Taiwan: A New History*. Routledge, London and New York. 1999.

Sanmao. *Stories of the Sahara*. Translated by Mike Fu. Bloomsbury Publishing, London. 2019.

Schubert, Gunter, and Jens Damm (eds.). *Taiwanese Identity in the Twenty-first Century: Domestic, Regional and Global Perspectives*. Routledge, London and New York. 2011.

Schubert, Gunter, and Chun-yi Lee (eds.). *Taiwan during the First Administration of Tsai Ing-wen: Navigating in Stormy Waters*. Routledge, London and New York, 2022.

Su Beng. *Taiwan's 400 Year History*: Anniversary Edition. SMC Publishing, Taipei. 2017.

Su Chi. *Taiwan's Relations with Mainland China: A Tail Wagging Two Dogs*. Routledge, London and New York. 2009.

Sullivan, Jonathan, and Lev Nachman. *Taiwan: A Contested Democracy under Threat*. Agenda Publishing, Newcastle upon Tyne. 2024.

Taylor, Jay. *The Generalissimo: Chiang Kai-shek and the Struggle for Modern China*. Belknap Press, Cambridge, MA. 2011.

Tien, Hung-mao. *The Great Transition: Political and Social Change in the Republic of China*. Hoover Institution Press, Stanford, CA. 1989.

Select Bibliography

Wedeman, Andrew. *Double Paradox: Rapid Growth and Rising Corruption in China*. Cornell University Press, Ithaca, NY, and London. 2012.

Wu, He. *Remains of Life*. Translated by Michael Berry. Columbia University Press, New York. 2017.

Wu, Ming-yi. *The Man with the Compound Eyes*. Translated by Darryl Sterk. Harvill Secker, London. 2013.

Wuthnow, Joel, Derek Grossman, Phillip C. Saunders, Andrew Scobell and Andrew N. D. Yang (eds.). *Crossing the Strait: China's Military Prepares for War with Taiwan*. National Defense University Press, Washington DC. 2022.

Yang, Dominic Meng-Hsuan. *The Great Exodus from China: Trauma, Memory, and Identity in Modern Taiwan*. Cambridge University Press, Cambridge. 2021.

Index

About the Author

KERRY BROWN is Professor of Chinese Studies and Director of the Lau China Institute at King's College, London. From 2012 to 2015 he was Professor of Chinese Politics and Director of the China Studies Centre at the University of Sydney. Prior to this he worked at Chatham House from 2006 to 2012, as Senior Fellow and then Head of the Asia Programme. From 1998 to 2005 he worked at the British Foreign and Commonwealth Office stationed in Beijing. He is the author of over twenty books on modern Chinese politics and his work has been translated into twelve languages.